Better means Better

Mark Curtis

ISBN 9798388901316
Printed in UK

Contents

Dedication

To all those who have walked with me over the years. Anything that has been accomplished has only been made possible through your faithfulness. Thank you!

Foreword

I have known Mark Curtis a few years now and it is a great privilege to endorse this very important book. Reading it was a great blessing for me.

Better surely means better, and The Holy Spirit has revealed, and used Mark to clearly show how much better the New Covenant is. We as the Body of Christ really need the open Heaven message that this book presents. Let us leave the Old Covenant behind with all its rules and regulations, and fully embrace the New Covenant, live in the freedom Christ won for us, and walk in love towards God and man. As you spend time reading this book, it will cause glory to shine on you.

I pray that your life will be changed, and forever blessed as you study the message found in this book.

Kim Torp

Pastor of Bible and Mission Centre Thisted Denmark

Leader of the Network Connections International Denmark

Introduction

This book has been in the making for a few years. For a long time I have noticed that parts of the charismatic church (I would unashamedly consider myself charismatic) have been filled with people who have pastoral issues in their lives that they consistently revisit and never seem to resolve. The answer to many of these issues isn't the laying on of hands and again I passionately believe in impartation and the miraculous. I've come to the conclusion that many of these issues could be sorted out through renewed thinking and a healthy understanding of who God is, what he has already done and what our identity is in him.

The basis of this is what the writer to the Hebrews referred to as the better covenant. Many people refer to the new covenant as a fuller more complete version of the old and as such use the terminology new covenant theology. The basis of this book is Hebrews 8 verse 6 which tells us there is a new covenant which is a better covenant. This book isn't primarily a theological work there are others who have written substantial works on this subject far better than I ever would. The heart behind this book is Pastoral written with a desire to put healthy foundations in peoples lives so that they can enjoy loving God, loving people and making a positive contribution to kingdom advancement.

The ideas here have grown out of the messages I've preached in recent years and a short course I offer to churches. My prayer is that you might grow in the freedom that is fully available to you in Christ.

Mark Curtis May 2023 Golborne UK

Understanding Covenants

It seems a sensible approach if we are examining the new covenant to look at the whole subject of covenants and how they relate together. It is important for us to make a distinction between the term old covenant and Old Testament. When we refer to the old covenant we are more accurately referring to the moral and ceremonial laws that were passed down through Moses. The old testament covers a period prior to this and in the new testament the law of Moses continued until Jesus died on the cross and cut a new covenant. This means that Jesus was living under the old covenant when he walked on earth. There is also a period that we refer to as a transitional period where both covenants were in place until A.D. 70 when the temple was destroyed and the ceremonial law finished. This is what the following verse is referring to

Hebrews 8 v 13

When He said, "A new covenant," He has made the first obsolete. But whatever is becoming obsolete and growing old is ready to disappear.

The old was made obsolete by the cross but was still waiting to disappear which is what happened with the destruction of the temple.

Understanding this distinction between old covenant and old testament helps us to interpret accurately passages like Galatians 4

Galatians 4 v 21 to 31

Tell me, you who want to be under law, do you not listen to the law? For it is written that Abraham had two sons, one by the

bondwoman and one by the free woman. But the son by the bondwoman was born according to the flesh, and the son by the free woman through the promise. This is allegorically speaking, for these women are two covenants: one proceeding from Mount Sinai bearing children who are to be slaves; she is Hagar. Now this Hagar is Mount Sinai in Arabia and corresponds to the present Jerusalem, for she is in slavery with her children. But the Jerusalem above is free; she is our mother.For it is written,
"Rejoice, barren woman who does not bear;
Break forth and shout, you who are not in labor;
For more numerous are the children of the desolate
Than of the one who has a husband."
And you brethren, like Isaac, are children of promise. But as at that time he who was born according to the flesh persecuted him who was born according to the Spirit, so it is now also. But what does the Scripture say? "Cast out the bondwoman and her son, For the son of the bondwoman shall not be an heir with the son of the free woman." So then, brethren, we are not children of a bondwoman, but of the free woman.
Here Paul is equating the law (old covenant) with Hagar and encourages us to throw it out. What we are throwing out is the system of rules and regulations not the old testament and in throwing it out we are embracing the freedom won for us in Christ.

In ancient times there were three types of covenant frequently used

1) Grant covenant

This is a non-conditional covenant where from a benevolent kind heart a ruler would bless a servant not on the grounds of any obedience but just from the generosity of his heart.

2) Kinship covenant

This was a covenant between two equal parties which was transactional in nature with both parties fulfilling separate conditions.

3) Vassal covenant

In a vassal covenant the king would establish many conditions that needed to be rigidly followed. The consequence of not following them would be death!

Four Covenants

In the old Testament there are four major covenants

1) Noah's Covenant

2) Abraham's Covenant

3) Moses Covenant

4) David's Covenant

Noah's Covenant

Genesis 9 verse 8 to 17

Then God spoke to Noah and to his sons with him, saying, "Now behold, I Myself do establish My covenant with you, and with your descendants after you; and with every living creature that is with you, the birds, the cattle, and every beast of the earth with you; of all that comes out of the ark, even every beast of the earth. I establish My covenant with you; and all flesh shall never again be cut off by the water of the flood, neither shall there again be a flood to destroy the earth." God said, "This is the sign of the covenant which I am making between Me and you and every living creature that is with you, for all successive generations; I set My bow in the cloud, and it shall be for a sign of a covenant between Me and the earth. It shall come about, when I bring a cloud over the earth, that the bow will be seen in the cloud, and I will remember My covenant, which is between Me and you and every living creature of all flesh; and never again shall the water become a flood to destroy all flesh. When the bow is in the cloud, then I will look upon it, to remember the everlasting covenant between God and every living creature of all flesh that is on the earth." And God said to Noah, "This is the sign of the covenant which I have established between Me and all flesh that is on the earth."

After the floodwaters have receded God makes an unconditional promise to Noah and his descendants that never again will the whole Earth be flooded. This covenantal promise is still in effect today!

Abraham's Covenant

Genesis 12 v 2 to 3

And I will make you a great nation,
And I will bless you,
And make your name great;
And so you shall be a blessing;
And I will bless those who bless you,
And the one who curses you I will curse.
And in you all the families of the earth will be blessed."

Abraham has an encounter with God that clearly changes his life forever and receives a covenant that is unconditional.

Amazingly even Abraham's failing with Hagar doesn't lead to God withdrawing his promise.

David's Covenant

In 2 Samuel 7 David is concerned about building a house for the Ark of the covenant. The Lord sees his heart and makes a covenantal promise to him.

2 Samuel 7 v 11 to 14, 16

even from the day that I commanded judges to be over My people Israel; and I will give you rest from all your enemies. The Lord also declares to you that the Lord will make a house for you. When your days are complete and you lie down with your fathers, I will raise up your descendant after you, who will come forth from you, and I will establish his kingdom. He shall build a house for My name, and I will establish the throne of his kingdom forever. I will be a father to him and he will be a son to Me; when he commits iniquity, I will correct him with the rod of men and the strokes of the sons of men
Again this covenant is totally unconditional.

In these three covenants we can see the heart of God expressed which is one of unconditional love where out of the goodness of his heart he simply wants to bless mankind. It is important to also note that Abraham's and David's covenant are both fulfilled in Jesus but that is another topic for another day!

Moses Covenant the old covenant

When we are referring to the old covenant what we are actually referring to is the covenant that God and Moses made. It is interesting to see the progression through the covenants with God and the nation of Israel.

Gods original intent

It has always been God's heart for man to know him and enjoy the intimacy of relationship. We see this in the garden of Eden before sin entered the world and we also see it in his subsequent covenant with Abraham. Things, however, take a different course as God seeks to make a covenant with the nation of Israel.

Before the Law is given on Mount Sinai

Exodus 19 verse 5 to 6 the Israelites grumbling led to no punishment

Exodus 16 verse 1 to 15 the Israelites grumbling about manna and quails led to no punishment

Exodus 16 verse 27 to 30 a sabbath violation resulted in no reprimand
Exodus 17 verse 1 to 7 the Israelites grumbling over water led to no punishment

After the law is given on Mount Sinai

Numbers 11 verse 1 to 3 grumbling led to a destructive fire

Numbers 11 verse 33 to 34 grumbling about manna and quails led to a killing plague

Numbers 15 verse 32 to 36 a sabbath violation resulted in death by stoning

Numbers 21 verse 46 the Israelites grumbling about water and food led to deadly serpents killing many

All the law ever produced was the inability of man to keep it and thereby live under its curse.

Here God is seeking to establish a covenant to bless them that fully reflects his heart. In it there is an invitation to the nation of Israel to become a nation of priests who can all know him in a direct relationship. The promise is that the whole Earth will be blessed through them. They turn away from this offer and ask Moses to represent them as a priest before God. This leads to the giving of the 10 Commandments on Mount Sinai which is reflective of a kinship covenant where both parties have to fulfil their part of the agreement. Everything is now conditional. Because of mans inability to receive God's unconditional love there is now a change in how God relates to the nation of Israel. Many people have wondered why the God of the old seems so different to the father that Jesus taught about. He is the same ! The story of the old is man's limited revelation of who God is. It is man making God in his own image.When we read the old in the revelation of the new we see he has always been loving and gracious.

Psalm 103 v 8

The Lord is compassionate and gracious,
Slow to anger and abounding in lovingkindness.

Paul makes a reference to this when he refers to the law being like a veil that hides our view of God as he really is.

2 Corinthians 3 v 14

But their minds were hardened; for until this very day at the reading of the old covenant the same veil remains unlifted, because it is removed in Christ

Here he outlines how a veil is drawn over God that only gets removed in Christ. Then we see him for who he really is. This is why the old covenant has to be done away with because it can't fully reflect Gods heart towards mankind. Gods offer of a covenant came fully from his heart but the covenant that was finally agreed was driven by the heart of man.

Unfolding Understanding

At the heart of understanding the new covenant is the realisation that whilst in eternity the plan of redemption was in its entirety established yet for humanity there is a gradual unfolding of that plan. We are told in the Bible that everything was in place before the foundation of the world.

Ephesians 1 v 4

Just as he chose us in him before the foundation of the world, that we will be holy and blameless before him

It is clear that man's understanding of God and his plan progresses throughout the Scriptures. This is also evident in the progression from the old covenant to the new covenant. The truth though is that the Lord has always remained the same

Malachi 3 v 6

For I, the Lord, do not change

His character is the same. He always has been gracious, compassionate and merciful. His heart has always been to enjoy intimacy with his people but the law put a veil over peoples understanding. This is why revelation appears progressive as it is based on man's understanding of God. What we're talking about here it's more about us than it is about God.

Types and shadows

In the book of Hebrews, which contains such a powerful unpacking of the new and better covenant, we see the writer contrast the substance and reality of the new with the type and shadow of the old. When you think about the shadow it is very different to reality. If you saw my shadow you would get a general outline of my shape but there will be no definition. You wouldn't know what colour my eyes are, the shape of my nose, my skin type, and whether I'm smiling or not. The shadow gives an idea but the real thing is so much better

Hebrews 10 v 1

For the law, since it has only a shadow of the good things to come and not the very form of things, can never, by the same sacrifices which they offer continually year by year, make perfect those who draw near.

The law was a shadow but Jesus is the reality. This is why the disciples on the road to Emmaus found their hearts burning with passion as Jesus unpacks the Scriptures to them. Here the shadow becomes a reality

Luke 24 v 32

They said to one another, were our hearts not burning within us while he was speaking to us on the road, while he was explaining the Scriptures to us?

What are the shadows?

There are so many wonderful insights that we can get in the types and shadows of the old. One area of controversy in the body of Christ surrounds the issue of festivals. There are many who feel very passionately that the festivals should be celebrated as part of our Jewish roots but what do we see taught in the new covenant?

Colossians 2 v16 to 17

Therefore no one is to act as your judge in regard to food or drink or in respect to a festival or a new moon or a Sabbath day - things which are a mere shadow of what is to come but the substance belongs to Christ

Here Paul, a Jew, who introduced Jesus to the Gentile world is very clear in his teaching. This isn't something where we place unnecessary burdens on others or use as a mark of superior spirituality. Why? Because the festivals are just shadows but the substance and reality is Jesus

The sabbath

The sabbath was instituted as a day of rest and the principle of rest is a good godly principle, however, the sabbath is just a shadow. Jesus is now the sabbath and there is a rest from our works because he did everything to reconcile us to the father. It isn't about what we do but all about what he has done.

Hebrews 4 v 9 to 10

So there remains a sabbath rest for the people of God. For the one who has entered his rest has himself also rested from his works, as God did from his.

The new and better covenant is a total replacement. Jesus is the reality! He is the high priest, Lamb of God, Hope of glory, our wisdom, our righteousness and our redemption.

When we look at the major festivals he is the fulfilment of them all. He is our Pentecost, our Passover and he has come to tabernacle with us.

What about the gospels?

Even in the gospel we see Jesus slowly introducing the new order and its teaching. He teaches a little but is still having to hold back revelation that is too much for old covenant minds to handle.

John 16 v 12 to 13

I have many more things to say to you, but you cannot bear them now. But when he, the spirit of truth, comes, He will guide you into all the truth for he will not speak of his own initiative, but whatever he hears he will speak and he will disclose to you what is to come

Here he indicates there are many things that he wants to say but when the Holy Spirit comes more revelation is received. We see this in the heavenly download Paul receives in his school of silence. Jesus ministered in the context of the old covenant (pre-the cross) whereas Paul ministered after the new covenant had been cut. This is important to know particularly when interpreting different Scriptures. One of the Scriptures that needs to be understood in its context is the following

Matthew 16 v 24 to 26

Then Jesus said to his disciples, if anyone comes after me he must deny himself and take up his cross and follow me.

This was before Jesus had died and we had died in him. I've met so many people who are sincere and devoted trying to do what Jesus has already done and the scriptural basis has been this verse, however, Galatians reminds us of what has already taken place.

Galatians 2 v 20

I've been crucified with Christ, and it is no longer I who live, but Christ lives in me and the life which I now live in the flesh I live by faith in the son of God, who loved me and gave himself up for me.

We have been crucified with him and the life of God now flows out of our lives! In all this the exciting truth that made the disciples hearts burn is that there is now a new covenant that is eternal where we become beneficiaries of everything that he has promised. No wonder it is called a better covenant.

Old or New or both?

The Bible is full of covenants, however, the principal ones we see are the old covenant and the new covenant.

Old covenant

In simple terms the old covenant was given to Moses and included what we refer to as the 10 commandments and over 613 different laws covering everything from acquiring Canaanite slaves to building fences on roofs. This was the covenant operated until Jesus fulfilled his mission.

New covenant

The new covenant was sealed by the shed blood of Jesus. When he died he cut a new covenant, we see this as Jesus takes communion with his disciples at the last supper.

Matthew 26 v 28

for this is My blood of the new covenant, which is poured out for many for forgiveness of sins.

The new covenant began at the cross and still applies today. Every believer would mentally ascent to the belief of the new covenant but it is apparent both in teaching and practice some hold to the belief that the two covenants old and new exist together in harmony. The new covenant isn't tagged onto the old covenant but instead replaces everything that existed before the old covenant was given until Christ came.

Galatians 3 v 24

Therefore the Law has become our tutor to lead us to Christ, so that we may be justified by faith

See how it reads in the amplified

with the result that the Law has become our tutor and our disciplinarian to guide us to Christ, so that we may be justified [that is, declared free of the guilt of sin and its penalty, and placed in right standing with God] by faith.

One of the churches we have ministered in many times are great at hospitality. They always invite us to a household so that we can enjoy the lunch. There was one particular household where a multitude of puddings would always be placed in front of us. We would then be asked the question which one would you like? Invariably the answer would be a little piece of everyone. Often when approaching the issue of the covenants our response is we want it all. We are inspired by all of what Jesus has done but would like to keep our trust in our own religious frameworks. The Bible as well as being the inspired word of God is the unfolding story of God's dealings with mankind, it has a beginning and an end and should be read in that context and not as a random pic and mix. Paul urged Timothy to rightly divide the word of God

2 Timothy 2 v 5

Be diligent to present yourself approved to God as a workman who does not need to be ashamed, accurately handling the word of truth.

The old covenant was based on the law of Moses and was valid until the cross. The new covenant started with the cross, resurrection, Ascension and outpouring of the Holy Spirit .

The writer to the Hebrews is very clear about this. He says the old covenant is obsolete

Hebrews 8 v 13

When He said, "A new covenant," He has made the first obsolete. But whatever is becoming obsolete and growing old is ready to disappear (vanish)

According to the dictionary the word obsolete means something that has fallen into disuse, has been discarded or is outmoded. In our everyday language we would say it is something that is done away with.

Vanishing away

Interesting that the language used is, it is getting ready to vanish away. Here the writer is speaking of a time in his near future when all the structures of the old covenant would be removed. This was what happened in A.D. 70 when the temple was destroyed as Jesus had spoken in Matthew 24

Matthew 24 v 1 to 4

Jesus came out from the temple and was going away when His disciples came up to point out the temple buildings to Him. And He said to them, "Do you not see all these things? Truly I say to you, not one stone here will be left upon another, which will not be torn down."
As He was sitting on the Mount of Olives, the disciples came to Him privately, saying, "Tell us, when will these things happen,

and what will be the sign of Your coming, and of the end of the age?"
And Jesus answered and said to them, "See to it that no one misleads you.

Matthew 24 v 34

Truly I say to you, this generation will not pass away until all these things take place.

The old covenant is over totally! Jesus is the only one who is sufficient. He has fulfilled the old covenant and is the Lamb of God who has removed/taken away our sins. No more sacrifices, religious rituals, works to please God but the good news is that Jesus has done it all that is why he declared it is finished. When we understand the chronology of what has taken place we understand the last days that Jesus was referring to. These are not the last days of time but the last days of the old covenant.

How do we approach the old covenant?

There is so much to learn from the old covenant but we are no longer to live there. It is full of types and shadows of Jesus which are no longer to be physically observed but they do teach us so much concerning Jesus, they have all now been fulfilled and he now is our Passover and our Pentecost. When we read the old covenant we now need to take it through the cross. As you read this book we will examine what this looks like in practical terms. I believe when we get a full understanding it has the power to liberate our lives and transform a relationship with the Lord.

Contrast in Covenants

Heaven is open

One of the wonderful things about journeying with the Lord is that our understanding doesn't remain static but that it grows and changes. For the early years of my ministry I held strong beliefs that the heavens were closed up by demonic forces operating in the heavenlies. The way to deal with these demonic forces was to fast and pray and make prophetic warfare declarations over a region or an area. The more diligent we would be the greater the breakthrough we would have. We would use terms like ' this is a hard place '. All of this led to a preoccupation with the demonic where in effect Jesus was rendered powerless (although we would never say that). The emphasis was on what we could do. If we prayed more, repented more, fasted more then things might change.

Key Bible verses that we used were Deuteronomy 28 v 23, Daniel 9 and 10, 2 Chronicles 7 v14 , Ephesians six v 12, and Isaiah 64 v 1 however, most of the time we used them with no reference to the finished work of Jesus.
Our intentions and heart were good and because the Lord is good he showed his kindness and grace to us but we were trapped in 2 covenants.

The crucial thing for us to understand in the better covenant is that the emphasis is on what Jesus has done and not on our human efforts.

So is heaven open?

The awesome good news is that heaven is open which is why the prayer Jesus taught his disciples can be fully answered 'your kingdom come your will be done on earth as it is in heaven'.

Under the old covenant there was the most holy place in the temple, the place where God wasn't accessible to ordinary people. Instead once a year the high priest would enter with blood from a sacrifice. There was a large curtain in the temple referred to as the veil which kept the holy place separate and inaccessible to anyone other than the high priest. Keeping in mind the high priest, the blood, the veil and the most holy place we can look at what Jesus accomplished at the cross. When Jesus our high priest shed his blood the veil in the temple was torn in two from top to bottom and the most holy place (heaven on Earth) was now available and accessible to all. Paul in his apostolic teachings and revelation consistently asked the churches to make Christ crucified central.

1 Corinthians 2v2

For I was determined to know nothing among you except Jesus Christ and Him crucified

This was because he knew the immense power of the cross. It is the pivotal moment in history filled with supernatural potency that changed everything in the universe. In a moment the barriers were removed and heaven became open. As the shedding of blood was complete so the veil was torn in two. No effort on our part, no religious activity, no trying to put things right. Jesus alone did it! He dealt with sin, the world and the powers of darkness and nothing could now stop heaven being open over our lives. Paul understood this when he made his amazing declaration

Romans 8 v 38 & 39

For I am convinced that neither death, nor life, nor angels, nor principalities, nor things present, nor things to come, nor powers, nor height, nor depth, nor any created thing, will be

able to separate us from the love of God which is in Christ Jesus.

When the veil was torn in two it wasn't a small partial act but it was total and complete. Heaven was now fully open. Interestingly, the veil was torn from top to bottom which was an indicator that God himself had removed the barrier. In scripture he is always seen as the initiator

1 John 4 v 19

We love, because he first loved us

He has opened heaven for us and no one can shut it.

Revelation 4 v 1

And behold I saw a door standing open in heaven.

When we realise this it changes how we operate and we fully understand our new position in Christ. No longer do we pray, sacrifice and give in order that Heaven might be opened but now we do all these things from the certain knowledge that heaven is open and we can experience the full extent of his love and the fullness of our inheritance. **Desire has now taken the place of duty.**

We no longer try to open heaven through our worship but now our worship is inspired by an open heaven. Everything has flipped! We now catch and carry his heart because we have total access to him.

Many times nowadays when I minister I will start my teaching session by thanking the Lord for an open heaven and invariably when I do this his presence starts to manifest. I remember on one occasion walking through Amsterdam airport and consciously thanking the Lord that there was an open heaven. I have to say it was one of the most precious and intimate times I have enjoyed with the Lord.

What is the fruit of an open heaven ?

I want to focus on just two Scriptures one from the Old Testament and one from the New Testament that will tell us something about how an open heaven can affect our lives. These were both prior to the cross when an open heaven was a temporary experience compared with the permanent blessing we have in the better covenant.

Ezekiel 1 v 1

The heavens were opened and I saw visions of God.

Here we see that Ezekiel's experience of an open heaven is that he has visions of God. It is a beautiful reminder that because now we are under a better covenant that we can readily experience God and see him for who he really is.

Mark 1v10 -11

He saw the heavens opened and the Spirit like a dove descending upon him and a voice came out of the heavens ' You are my beloved son, in you I am well pleased

This is a story of Jesus being baptised . It tells us the heavens were opened and the Holy Spirit came upon him in the form of a dove . Then the Father speaks from heaven the words ' you are my beloved son in whom I am well pleased'. It is interesting to note that this experience is before Jesus embarked on his ministry, he had done nothing at this stage to win approval but the Father loved him for who he is and not what he had done. It is good to know that in the better covenant that we now live under there is a permanent open heaven and our Father is speaking words of approval over our lives. He loves us not for what we do but for who we are. We are his children made in his image and nothing can ever separate us from his love.

All of this gives us a foundation of security now we have our focus on him and not the powers of darkness. Someone once said to me many years ago if you have a large Jesus then you will have a small devil. When we live in the finished work of Jesus and enjoy the access we have to him this will totally change how we live and how we minister.

Saints not sinners

I remember many years ago being in a small group gathering in someone's house. As we shared our various perspectives I mentioned that I believed we could live a day without sinning and often days will pass without me having to confess sin in my life. As a young relatively inexperienced person I was shocked by the response that came my way 'you are a heretic to say you can live without sin'. Sadly over the years I've come to understand that this is a viewpoint held by many. It is common to hear people use terminology like we are sinners saved by Grace

So let's ask the question are we sinners or are we saints? This is a fundamental question because what we believe about our identity will determine how we live our lives.

Proverbs 23 v 7

For as he thinks within himself, so he is.

The old problem

The problem of humanity was the sin problem. We lived with a sinful nature (the body of sin) that resulted in sinful behaviour. The old covenant reminded us of our sinfulness and could only provide a covering for our sin. In fact the word atonement literally means a covering. We were told that the human heart was deceitfully wicked (Jeremiah) and we were prisoners unable to break free from this wickedness. Thankfully the story doesn't end there as that would be incredibly depressing. There is good news. Even in the old we prophetically see the promise of the new.

Ezekiel 36v26

Moreover, I will give you a new heart and put a new spirit within you; and I will remove the heart of stone from your flesh and give you a heart of flesh. I will put My Spirit within you and cause you to walk in My statutes,

There is now a glorious freedom in Christ that includes not only freedom from the guilt that sin infers but a freedom from the power of sin. Our salvation isn't a patch up job but it's a radical transformation.

2 Corinthians 5 v 19

Therefore if anyone is in Christ, he is a new creature; the old things passed away; behold, new things have come.

We are new creations, the old hasn't gone in part but has gone completely and the new is now resident in our lives.

1 Corinthians 15 v 22

For as in Adam all die, so also in Christ all will be made alive.

The key to understanding this transaction is to remember that we are in Christ. In Romans 6 it tells us that we were included in the death, burial and resurrection of Jesus. When he died our old man, our sinful nature was nailed to the cross with him. When he was buried we too were buried (this is what baptism signifies) and when he rose again we were raised to new life. The power of the cross isn't substitution but identification. Jesus didn't die in our place for we died with him.

knowing this, that our old self was crucified with Him, in order that our body of sin might be done away with, so that we would no longer be slaves to sin; for he who has died is freed from sin.

Sins power has been totally broken in our lives. We are set free from sin, we are no longer slaves to sin but we are united in the likeness of the resurrection of Jesus. We have received eternal life which is far more than immortality ie:- our ability to live forever. The Greek word for eternal life is Zoe which literally means God's kind of life. We now have the capacity to be like him, to talk like him, to think like him, and to live like him.

Dual natures

One of the teachings that is prevalent is the viewpoint that we have two natures, the old nature and the new nature. One passage that is often referenced is Romans seven where Paul the apostle talks about doing what he doesn't want to do and not doing what he does want to do. The key to understanding this scripture is examining the context. In Romans six Paul paints a picture of the freedom that Grace has brought to us in Christ. Then in chapter 7 he contrasts it with the law which was good but only reminds us of our inability to break free from sin, however, Romans eight reminds us of the solution. Many people spend their lives trying to kill their old man. I remember years ago knowing a young guy whose chat up line was ' I am dying '........needless to say he was unsuccessful in his pursuit of the young woman . How can you kill something that is already dead. Sometimes the words of Jesus are quoted and we are encouraged to take up our cross and deny ourselves by dying daily. The only problem is this was spoken before the cross. When Jesus died we died too and our old man is now (past tense) dead. We are actually exhorted to consider ourselves dead to sin but alive to God through Jesus. What an awesome gospel!

Romans 8 v 1-3

Therefore there is now no condemnation for those who are in Christ Jesus. For the law of the Spirit of life in Christ Jesus has set you free from the law of sin and of death. For what the Law could not do, weak as it was through the flesh, God did:

What the law couldn't do God did through Jesus. A new law is at work in us , it's the law of the Spirit of life in Christ. The old has gone and the new has come. If people hold to a classical view of the afterlife i.e. heaven and hell lets ask the question where does the old nature go and where does the new nature go.

What about sin ?

It is fair to ask the question about believers sinning, so where does that sin come from? Man is a triune being made in the image of God three in one. He has spirit, soul and body. Sin is no longer an issue of nature (our spirit) as we are no longer sinners. It is an issue of soul and body. The soul is the seat of the emotions and mind. Sin occurs in a believers life when our thinking isn't renewed. It is critical we address our thinking. When we have a sin consciousness all that will produce in our lives is sin. A few years ago I was teaching in a pastors conference where the teaching challenged sin consciousness. People were shocked when I happened to share that if you preach on adultery every week you will produce adultery in the church. If ,however, we preach Jesus and his gospel revolution we will see people start to live like Jesus. This is what I call Jesus consciousness. Scripture encourages us to do just that.

Colossians 3 v 2

Set your mind on the things above, not on the things that are on earth. For you have died and your life is hidden with Christ in God.

The key to transformation is to renew our thought patterns. To allow the word of Christ to dwell in us richly. We don't just think about Jesus but now we think like him.

Romans 12 v 1 to 2

Therefore I urge you, brethren, by the mercies of God, to present your bodies a living and holy sacrifice, acceptable to God, which is your spiritual service of worship. And do not be conformed to this world, but be transformed by the renewing of your mind, so that you may prove what the will of God is, that which is good and acceptable and perfect.

Partakers of the divine nature

2 Peter 1v4

For by these He has granted to us His precious and magnificent promises, so that by them you may become partakers of the divine nature, having escaped the corruption that is in the world by lust

We are new creations. We are part of a brand-new human race that is like the second Adam Jesus who is referred to as a life-giving spirit. We too, as we release the life that is in us become life givers. This was always God's plan that man would live from the tree of life and not the tree of the knowledge of good and evil. Right and wrong was never in his heart but life was. It is that life within us that produces holiness and goodness.

What is the divine nature?

We see this expressed very simply

1 John 4 v 8

God is Love

Love isn't an attribute of God but it is who he is. It is the divine nature and we see it described beautifully in Paul's letter to the Corinthians.

1 Corinthians 13 v 4 to 13

Love is patient, love is kind and is not jealous; love does not brag and is not arrogant, does not act unbecomingly; it does not seek its own, is not provoked, does not take into account a wrong suffered, does not rejoice in unrighteousness, but rejoices with the truth; bears all things, believes all things, hopes all things, endures all things.Love never fails; but if there are gifts of prophecy, they will be done away; if there are tongues, they will cease; if there is knowledge, it will be done away.For we know in part and we prophesy in part; but when the perfect comes, the partial will be done away. When I was a child, I used to speak like a child, think like a child, reason like a child; when I became a man, I did away with childish things. For now we see in a mirror dimly, but then face to face; now I know in part, but then I will know fully just as I also have been fully known. But now faith, hope, love, abide these three; but the greatest of these is love.

As we remind ourselves of our true identity so we start to live out of the divine nature.

SO A SAINT YOU ARE!

We are changed people with a changed identity. When Paul the Apostle is writing to the believers at Corinth he brings out a list of terrible sins that had been committed. These included fornication, idolatry, adultery, stealing and drunkenness, however, that is now past. Instead he declares their new identity

1 Corinthians 13 v 4 to 13

Such were some of you; but you were washed, but you were sanctified, but you were justified in the name of the Lord Jesus Christ and in the Spirit of our God.

Sin is completely broken!

Romans 6 v 14

For sin shall not be master over you, for you are not under law but under grace.

Sin is no longer our master but Jesus is. Gerald Coates the British church leader tells the story of someone who spoke with him. They said they couldn't live a day without sinning, when Gerald asked them Can you live one hour without sinning ? no came the reply. How about a minute, still the reply was no. Well how about a second, eventually the reply came yes ! Gerald then said the secret to living a day without sinning is to live second by second.

Part of our growth and maturity is that we learn to live from our new identity so that sinning is no longer a part of our daily life. John's epistle reminds us if we sin not when we sin, it is now the exception and not the rule.

1 John 1 v 9

If we confess our sins, He is faithful and righteous to forgive us our sins and to cleanse us from all unrighteousness.

This is why John teaches us to believe that we will not sin as we learn to abide in Christ.

1 John 3:6, 9

"No one who abides in Him sins; no one who sins has seen Him or knows Him. . . . No one who is born of God practices sin, because His seed abides in him; and he cannot sin, because he is born of God"

This is the incredible radical transformative nature of the gospel! No wonder our boast is in the cross. He finished it all and his victory over sin is complete.

Guilty or Innocent

Right at the very heart of this discussion between the two covenants is the issue of guilt and condemnation. I know in the early days of my Christian life I would struggle a great deal with feelings of guilt. I knew the Lord and I was very zealous for him but no matter how hard I tried I struggled with guilty feelings of failure . The more effort I put into disciplining myself and developing little rules of my life such as more prayer or filling my life with lots of religious activity it only served to compound my dilemma. I'm so grateful that the Lord is patient and that he turned a switch on in my life so that little by little I got a revelation of all that Jesus had accomplished at the cross. A number of years ago I was ministering in a leaders seminar when I told those present that we weren't called to preach about sin as that will only produce sin but that our call is to preach Jesus so that we produce Jesus in peoples lives. Needless to say not everyone appreciated the comment. It highlighted to me how much of our preaching in church is about sin and behaviour modification and not the transformative nature of the Gospel. So how does God see things from his perspective

Our sins are forgiven, taken away and forgotten

All of our sins past, present and future were forgiven when Jesus died 2,000 years ago

Colossians 2 v 13

When you were dead in your transgressions and the uncircumcision of your flesh, He made you alive together with Him, having forgiven us all our transgressions,

Colossians 1 v 13 & 14

For He rescued us from the domain of darkness, and transferred us to the kingdom of His beloved Son, in whom we have redemption, the forgiveness of sins.

The word forgiven is the Greek word aphesis. It means a release from bondage , a sending away, the cancelling of all punishment, obligation or debt. Wow ! What Jesus did is fully comprehensive. His one sacrifice is sufficient! The blood he shared is for everyone it really is a finished work.

Hebrews 10 v 12

but He, having offered one sacrifice for sins for all time, sat down at the right hand of God

In the old covenant our sins were covered but in the new covenant they are totally removed fulfilling the prophetic declaration that John the Baptist made concerning Jesus

John 1 v 29

The next day he saw Jesus coming to him and *said, "Behold, the Lamb of God who takes away the sin of the world!

Jesus didn't come into the world to make the world feel more guilty but to reconcile the world back to his father. It is a ministry of reconciliation not condemnation.

2 Corinthians 5 v 18 & 19

Now all these things are from God, who reconciled us to Himself through Christ and gave us the ministry of reconciliation, namely, that God was in Christ reconciling the world to Himself, not counting their trespasses against them, and He has committed to us the word of reconciliation.

The truth is that God is for us and not against us. This is our message it is that the father sent Jesus so that we could be reconciled.

Romans 8 v 1

Therefore there is now no condemnation for those who are in Christ Jesus.

There is no condemnation, there is no guilt! We are now reconciled. Often we can feel great feelings of condemnation. It is not the Lord who is condemning us. There is only one accuser and that is the devil. I often say he sits on our shoulders whispering condemnation in our ears. We overcome his accusations by reminding him that the blood of Jesus has dealt with every sin, every thought, word and deed we have ever had and ever will is totally forgiven and we are fully free from guilt.

Revelation 12 v 10 & 11

Now the salvation, and the power, and the kingdom of our God and the authority of His Christ have come, for the accuser of our brethren has been thrown down, he who accuses them before our God day and night. And they overcame him because of the blood of the Lamb and because of the word of their testimony, and they did not love their life even when faced with death.

Fully righteous

What is righteousness and how does God view it. Is it something we receive or something we work for ? If you were to ask someone are you fully holy or fully righteous usually you will be met by a response of embarrassment. It's almost as if you were to say that you are righteous you would demonstrate that you aren't because to say such a thing would reveal pride. It almost seems that we have more confidence in ourselves than we do in Jesus and what he accomplished. True humility is agreeing with what he says and how he views us,

What is righteousness?

1) Right standing

2) The ability to stand in the presence of the father as though sin had never existed and without any sense of guilt shame or inferiority.

It is amazing how we try to be righteous but all we reveal is a sense of self righteousness where we think we are better than others and we are more concerned about what we think and what others think of us. Self-righteousness always produces two things in our lives. The first of these is pride and the second is condemnation. In Luke 15 Jesus tells the story of the rich man and the sinner . The prayer of the religious man reveals his true heart as he compares himself with the sinner. Comparison is always at the heart of self righteousness. We see self-righteousness in evidence again in the story of the Prodigal son. As the Father welcomes his wayward son home, the older brother complains that he is being faithful and working hard in service of his father. When we are self-righteous our emphasis is on our work and service where the fathers emphasis has always been on relationship.

Righteousness is a gift

Philippians 3 v 9

that I may gain Christ, and may be found in Him, not having a righteousness of my own derived from the Law, but that which is through faith in Christ, the righteousness which comes from God on the basis of faith,

This is the wonder of the gospel. Our righteousness is not worked for, is not paid for or earned but it is a free gift. How wonderful! We didn't become sinners solely because of our disobedience but it was Adams disobedience. In the same way we don't become righteous because of our obedience but because of Jesus and his shed blood .

Romans 5 v 19

For as through the one man's disobedience the many were made sinners, even so through the obedience of the One the many will be made righteous.

Right at the heart of this is our understanding of how God views us. Often we have taught that God separates himself from us because of our sin but the first thing that Adam does when he sins is to withdraw and hide. God knows where he is hiding but still asks the question where are you? He reveals his longing for relationship with man. Separation really is an illusion. No wonder Paul the Apostle proclaims that nothing can separate us from his love and that includes your feelings of condemnation.

Romans 8 v 38 & 39

For I am convinced that neither death, nor life, nor angels, nor principalities, nor things present, nor things to come, nor powers, nor height, nor depth, nor any other created thing, will be able to separate us from the love of God, which is in Christ Jesus our Lord.

He took our sin so we could receive his righteousness.

2 Corinthians 5v21

He made Him who knew no sin to be sin on our behalf, so that we might become the righteousness of God in Him.

What do we do to become righteous?

It is simple......believe and receive! In the old covenant the predominant way of thinking was behave and obey whereas in the new covenant it is believe and receive. This is a good way to discover whether we are operating from the old or the new. Righteousness is a gift where we simply receive and by simple faith is how we receive it.

Romans 10v10

for with the heart a person believes, resulting in righteousness, and with the mouth he confesses, resulting in salvation.

Romans 3v22

even the righteousness of God through faith in Jesus Christ for all those who believe; for there is no distinction

Romans 3v24

being justified as a gift by His grace through the redemption which is in Christ Jesus;

The Great Exchange

The cross covers it all. A divine exchange took place

From sin to righteousness
From sickness to healing
From shame to honour
From curse to blessing
From rejection to acceptance
From poverty to riches

Sons not Servants

We have seen already that there is a progression of revelation in scripture of who God is and what our relationship is to him now. In the old covenant the predominant thinking is that he was primarily Almighty God and our relationship to him was that of a servant obeying the master. In the new covenant we see that the primary revelation Jesus came to bring was an understanding that God relates to us as a father, therefore, our relationship with him is that of a father and his son. In short our identity is that of sons and not servants.

Ephesians 1 v 5

He predestined us to adoption as sons with Jesus Christ

Romans 8 v v 15 and 16

For you have not received a spirit of slavery leading to fear again, but you have received a spirit of adoption as sons by which we cry out, "Abba! Father!" The Spirit Himself testifies with our spirit that we are children of God, and if children, heirs also, heirs of God and fellow heirs with Christ,

Galatians 3 v 26

For you are all sons of God through faith in Christ Jesus

John 1 v 12

But as many as received Him, to them He gave the right to become children of God, even to those who believe in His name,

Relationship

To fully embrace this identity we have as sons we need to settle in our hearts that the father is totally committed to relationship. The Trinity is such a beautiful picture of God's commitment to relationship. We are the object of his desire and he is constant in his pursuit of us. In fact the word relentless would demonstrate the full passion of this pursuit. Many years ago there was a famous book called the God Chasers. I understood the heart of the book which was an encouragement for people to be zealous in their pursuit of God and his ways but if I'm honest the title used to niggle me. The more I thought about it, the more certain I was that my story and the story of humanity is the story of the Man Chaser. Whilst religion has instilled a mentality of duty in us the father still reaches out to us to free us from our efforts to please him. The bottom line is that he is pleased with us because we are his. When the fullness came with Jesus we started to understand that we could never escape the grip of his love, we were included in him before the world began perhaps one of the most powerful illustrations of the fathers heart is the story of the Prodigal son. It is interesting that we give the story that title because really it is the story of the fathers heart. We read the story in

Luke 15 v 11 to 32

Then he said, "There was once a man who had two sons. The younger said to his father, 'Father, I want right now what's coming to me.'
"So the father divided the property between them. It wasn't long before the younger son packed his bags and left for a distant country. There, undisciplined and dissipated, he wasted everything he had. After he had gone through all his money, there was a bad famine all through that country and he began to hurt. He signed on with a citizen there who assigned him to

his fields to slop the pigs. He was so hungry he would have eaten the corncobs in the pig slop, but no one would give him any.

"That brought him to his senses. He said, 'All those farmhands working for my father sit down to three meals a day, and here I am starving to death. I'm going back to my father. I'll say to him, Father, I've sinned against God, I've sinned before you; I don't deserve to be called your son. Take me on as a hired hand.' He got right up and went home to his father.

"When he was still a long way off, his father saw him. His heart pounding, he ran out, embraced him, and kissed him. The son started his speech: 'Father, I've sinned against God, I've sinned before you; I don't deserve to be called your son ever again.'

"But the father wasn't listening. He was calling to the servants, 'Quick. Bring a clean set of clothes and dress him. Put the family ring on his finger and sandals on his feet. Then get a grain-fed heifer and roast it. We're going to feast! We're going to have a wonderful time! My son is here—given up for dead and now alive! Given up for lost and now found!' And they began to have a wonderful time.

"All this time his older son was out in the field. When the day's work was done he came in. As he approached the house, he heard the music and dancing. Calling over one of the houseboys, he asked what was going on. He told him, 'Your brother came home. Your father has ordered a feast— barbecued beef!—because he has him home safe and sound.' "The older brother stalked off in an angry sulk and refused to join in. His father came out and tried to talk to him, but he wouldn't listen. The son said, 'Look how many years I've stayed here serving you, never giving you one moment of grief, but have you ever thrown a party for me and my friends? Then this son of yours who has thrown away your money on whores shows up and you go all out with a feast!' "His father said, 'Son, you don't understand. You're with me all the time, and everything that is mine is yours—but this is a wonderful time, *and we had to celebrate. This brother of yours was dead, and he's alive! He was lost, and he's found!'"*

Fathers heart

Here we see the fathers heart throughout the story. He is giving everything to his sons not based on their performance but on their relationship with him. They are his sons!

The Sons speech

When the wayward son comes to his senses he prepares his speech that he will deliver to his father. It went something like this I have sinned against God, I have sinned against you, I don't deserve to be your son take me on as one of your servants. Wow, how many times have we maybe prayed a similar prayer. Maybe when we have messed up we have said to the Lord if you forgive me I'll serve you more faithfully, I'll pray more, read my bible more, witness more, give more. But what is the Fathers response.

The fathers response

I love the Fathers response, In verse 22 it puts it very bluntly. It says that the father wasn't listening! When we pray our servant prayers he is deaf to it because the sound he responds to is the sound of desire and not duty. Desire springs from a devotion of heart and a love of intimacy whereas duty is nurtured in a place of religion and obligation. The father demonstrates his heart by responding in four ways.

Love and Affection

There is such a beautiful revelation of Gods heart towards his children even when we have been wayward and rebellious. The first thing we see is that the father spots the son from a long way off. You get the feeling that every day he's looking down the road in the hope that his son returns. The first glimpse he gets of the sons return and he is running down the road to greet him. We are told that he embraces and kisses him. The universal language of love. O how he loves us! God is not a cold distant force but he is a loving father committed to his children. He longs to embrace us and hold us in his arms.

A new robe

The son had returned dirty, filled with shame, most likely semi naked. The first thing the father does is clean him and cover him. The joy of restoration is this that every sin, every trace of guilt, every exposure and shame is cleansed and removed. We now have a new set of clothes for life called a robe of righteousness. We are now totally free and have right standing (restored relationship) with the father and this extends to our relationship with each other and even with ourselves.

A family ring

The second act was putting the family ring on his finger. This was a reminder of two powerful things.

Identity

He belonged to his father, he was part of the family that extends both backwards and forwards in time. He was part of the community founded upon unconditional love. This is our story, we are connected in relationship with our father but also a part of the wider family. This is both the church which is a mysterious community spanning the nations and also the human family that derives its name from the father.

Ephesians 4v14 to 15

For this reason I bow my knees before the Father, from whom every family in heaven and on earth derives it's name.

Authority

I have a good friend Joseph Mwila who comes from Zambia in southern Africa. One day Joseph shared with me the importance of rings in African culture. He explained how many powerful leaders would wear a ring that symbolised their power and authority. If they were in a meeting they would often turn the ring on their finger as a reminder to others they were in control. What a beautiful picture of the ring we receive as reconciled sons. We also carry power and authority, actually we carry the same authority that Jesus has. This authority is given to us in the name of Jesus which Phillipians tells us is the name above all of the names. That's why we read ;

Mark 16v 17 to 18

These signs will accompany those who have believed: in My name they will cast out demons, they will speak with new tongues; they will pick up serpents, and if they drink any deadly poison, it will not hurt them; they will lay hands on the sick, and they will recover.

It's not a partial restoration but one that is total and complete.

Sandals

In ancient traditions it was footwear that distinguished servants from sons. Most servants were barefooted but sons had sandals. In this one act the father reminds the son that you were always my son and always will be my son. Our father has made the same commitment to us. We will never be servants but always sons enjoying the privilege of relationship and the wonder of an amazing inexhaustible inheritance.

Mixed up thinking

It's amazing how easily we can slip into old covenant thinking and speaking. On many occasions scripture urges us not to be double minded in our thinking.

I had the privilege of being part of an apostolic roundtable with other apostolic leaders from around the world. There were many thought-provoking conversations during our time together. On one occasion one of the leaders made a slightly casual remark that made me think. He spoke of how many people have been blessed through the revelation of the fathers heart and yet were still struggling with issues of insecurity having a fear of encountering the Lord's displeasure, All of this contributed to many people living as emotional cripples. Yet when we truly know the fathers love it has to be amongst the most liberating truths we can encounter in the universe. I've reflected on this comment often and I'm convinced that most of it has in its foundation mixed up thinking. Religious, servant mentality coupled with old covenant views of God will systematically erode our confidence in the fathers love. We're not talking about tagging the new onto the old because when Jesus established a new covenant it was a better covenant. It is a total replacement job. New really means new!

Benefits of Sonship

Security

Sadly in life many of us have had difficult experiences involving broken relationships often accompanied by feelings of rejection and betrayal. This becomes a breeding ground in our hearts and minds for harmful emotions. Often we start to live with an expectation that relationships will not work out and that we will constantly experience rejection in our lives. It is a tragedy that many encounter the father in his love but even in that encounter wonder if it is too good to be true. Then if we are exposed to old covenant thinking particularly those centred around our human performance e.g. theologies of blessings and curses and a view of Almighty God who is waiting to punish sinners then these feelings become compounded. The result of this is insecurity. The truth is so very different our father doesn't walk out on us. In fact we could never be closer than what we are! We are now in him and he is in us! We have the security that we are eternally united with him. No place for fear or insecurity we will always belong to him. We couldn't be any more qualified than we are and it's all because of his grace. We can now enjoy our daddy knowing that we are his delight!

Status

Slaves have no status and no authority. They are told what to do and what not to do but children have the privilege of belonging and being able to enjoy family privileges. My two daughters are now adult and live away but when they come to visit us they don't ask where they can sit, they go to the fridge without invitation, they choose their own TV shows, why because they belong, they're in the family house. They have the status of daughters and everything belongs to them. It is the same for us, we can enjoy our fathers world knowing we have the status of being his children. There is such a trend in the Church to give ourselves a title and confer status upon ourselves but how wonderfully liberating it is to know that we are his children and he loves us dearly. What greater status can we have than that of being children of God.

1 John 3 v 1

See how great a love the Father has bestowed on us, that we would be called children of God; and such we are

Intimacy

In Romans 8 it tells us that we now cry Abba father. The word Abba isn't a formal word but in our setting it would be like the term dad or daddy. This isn't a formal relationship we are in devoid of love but instead one of warmth, tenderness and affection. In response to his great love we are drawn into a place of intimacy with the maker of heaven and earth who is a daddy. We enjoy his embrace and from the depths of our being love him.

Inheritance

All wise parents will make provision for their children for when they are no longer alive. One of the most powerful ways we can know we are sons of God is our inheritance. We are now joint heirs with Jesus who is our elder brother. When we pause for a moment to allow that to sink in we realise this is totally mind blowing. So what do we inherit ?

The best way to discover our inheritance is to ask the question what did Jesus inherit?

The nations

In Psalm 2 we have an intriguing conversation in the godhead where the father says to the son 'ask of me'.

Psalm 2 v 8

*Ask of Me, and I will surely give the nations as Your inheritance,
And the very ends of the earth as Your possession.*

Lost humanity belongs to him as do the nations of the world.
Remember that this is the temptation that the devil brought
Jesus in the wilderness. Jesus was totally secure in his fathers
love and in the knowledge that the nations would become his.
Security enables destinies to be realised. Jesus knew that
through his death, burial and resurrection that the nations will
become his possession. This is what the book of Revelation is
speaking about

Revelation 11 v 15

*The kingdom of the world has become the kingdom of our
Lord and of His Christ; and He will reign forever and ever.*

Whatever belongs to him belongs to us that is why we are
passionate about the nations it is because they are our
inheritance as joint heirs. In the finished work of Jesus it is
already done, the nations are his but through the ministry of
the church the kingdom is established in real, visible and
tangible terms

Authority

We have already touched on this a little bit.

Matthew 28 v 18

*And Jesus came up and spoke to them, saying, "All authority
has been given to Me in heaven and on earth. Go therefore*

and make disciples of all the nations, baptizing them in the name of the Father , the Son and the Holy Spirit

It is clear that all authority has been given to Jesus and that we have received all the authority that has been given to Jesus. This is what John G Lake the apostolic leader of the 20th century referred to as the strongman's gospel. There may be times we feel weak but those feelings are a poor commentary of the truth. The gospel message is the message of the King and his kingdom. This kingdom is ever growing, ever-increasing, there are no limits to it's authority. We see this prophesied through Isaiah who declared of the increase of his government and his peace there will be no end. Things are getting better. The whole earth will be filled with the knowledge of God. This authority is ours too because we are in Christ

Romans 5 v 17

For if by the transgression of the one, death reigned through the one, much more those who receive the abundance of grace and of the gift of righteousness will reign in life through the One, Jesus Christ.

2 Corinthians 2 v 14

But thanks be to God, who always leads us in triumph in Christ, and manifests through us the sweet aroma of the knowledge of Him in every place.

We were created to reign in life and know dominion. His victory is always. He is never defeated. I often refer to him as the undisputed champion of the world. He takes the weak and foolish and turns them into the strong and wise. This is now our inheritance to know his victory and the authority he has given us.

Glory

The one we honour and worship is the glorious one filled with glory. There are many Scriptures which remind us of the glory that Jesus has

Hebrews 1 v 3

And He is the radiance of His glory and the exact representation of His nature, and upholds all things by the word of His power.

2 Peter 1 v 17

For when He received honor and glory from God the Father, such an utterance as this was made to Him by the Majestic Glory, "This is My beloved Son with whom I am well-pleased"

It is almost impossible to define the word glory and convey the enormity of what it is. In scripture there are two words used. Firstly there is the Hebrew word kabod which means heaviness or weight. It's a term that was often used in assessing the worth and value of precious stones. In fact it is referring to the infinite worth and value that belongs to Jesus and is summed up beautifully in the words of the song
Lord you are more precious than silver
Lord you are more costly than gold
Lord you are more beautiful than diamonds
And nothing on this earth compares to you

The second word we use is the Greek word doxa from which we get our English term doxology. Doxa means to declare or speak out, it is the speaking out of the wonder of who God is, again connected to his worth and value. Most often when we think of glory we have in our minds the breathtaking splendour of who God is, the perfection of his being and the completeness of his many faceted attributes. This is the mysterious wonder of the father now seen in Jesus. It is his perfection. In John 17 we read a truly outrageous statement by Jesus

John 17 v 22

The glory which You have given Me I have given to them, that they may be one, just as We are one

The very same glory Jesus has received from the father has now been given to us. When we think of the wonder of his glory and then the realisation that is what we have received it is truly more than we can fully comprehend. It is the glorious nature of the new creation in Christ where we are made not only in his image but also in his likeness.

Amazing Grace

One of the most famous hymns of all time is amazing grace. When we consider what grace is and what it does we can see what an apt title this is. Grace really is truly amazing!

There is no doubt that the whole topic of grace has stirred up controversy in recent years. It isn't a rare thing to be asked 'are you one of those grace preachers?' or 'are you into hyper grace?'. The whole book of Galatians is effectively given over to contrasting a false gospel based on law and works whereas the true gospel is based on grace, faith and life in the spirit. To put it succinctly grace is the gospel!

1) Grace embraces

The wonder of the gospel is that through the cross God extends his grace towards humanity. Bill hybels put it powerfully when he's said 'you will never set eyes on anyone who doesn't matter to God'. Sometimes people use the term cheap grace, however, there is no such thing. Grace is incredibly costly. Many people with religious mindsets believe that through penance and suffering more or sacrificing more they can pay the price for their sin. The truth is that all our sacrifice still can't pay the price. There is only one who could pay the price so that we can freely receive all things by grace. The blood of Jesus is all sufficient and is valuable enough to buy every person on the planet.

1 Peter 1 v 18 to 19

knowing that you were not redeemed with perishable things like silver or gold from your futile way of life inherited from your forefathers, but with precious blood, as of a lamb unblemished and spotless, the blood of Christ.

It isn't cheap but it is free! If I was to give you a Lexus car as a gift it would be free to you but it would involve paying an expensive price. That is what happened at the cross, grace is the administration of all that he has given peace, love, Joy, forgiveness, eternal life, righteousness and much more. Grace is precious and valuable and free to all. There isn't a single person beyond the reach of his grace. When we understand grace we start to realise how offensive it is to religious self-righteousness! As the hymn describes it:- 'The vilest offender who truly believes that moment from Jesus a pardon receives'.

Grace can reach the murderer, the terrorist, the rapist as well as the sophisticated respectable sinner.

Grace transforms

When we start preaching on grace many people will argue that grace isn't a license to sin. In effect what these people mean is that we were saved by grace but we are made righteous through obeying the law. We need to remind ourselves that we are saved by grace, transformed by grace, kept by grace , and presented complete before the father by grace. It is all the work of grace in our lives. At its heart grace is a person whose name is Jesus.

John 1 v 14

And the Word became flesh, and dwelt among us, and we saw His glory, glory as of the only begotten from the Father, full of grace and truth

John 1 v 17

For the Law was given through Moses; grace and truth were realized through Jesus Christ.

When Jesus came he revealed his father. He was the physical embodiment of God. In the old Testament we get insights into his character and nature.

Psalm 145 v 8

The Lord is gracious and merciful;
Slow to anger and great in lovingkindness.

Psalm 145 v 17

The Lord is righteous in all His ways
And kind in all His deeds.

When this revelation moves beyond our minds and into the core of our being we realise that only grace can fully transform us.

Titus 2 v 11 to 12

For the grace of God has appeared, bringing salvation to all men, instructing us to deny ungodliness and worldly desires and to live sensibly, righteously and godly in the present age,

This changes the way we disciple people. No more do we try to impose change through external rules and regulations but we allow grace to do its work. It teaches us to say no to all ungodliness!

A number of years ago I was preaching the gospel and at the end of my message I gave an appeal for people to receive salvation. Amongst those who responded there was a couple who were living together as a non-married couple. A few weeks later the pastor spoke with me about this couple conscious they were 'living in sin' and wanting a viewpoint on how to approach the situation. I had been observing this couple and it was evident that they had experienced a genuine encounter with the Lord. You could see they were growing, changing, and opening up to the Lord. My advice to the pastor was to say nothing and allow the Holy Spirit (grace) to do his work. Short time after the man approached his pastor saying I've been reading the bible and I notice that it talks about fornication, is this what I'm doing? They were able to have a gentle open conversation about this that led to the couple getting married and over time they became an important part of the church. If we had stepped in applying the law they most likely would have been offended, hardened their hearts and backslid , however, allowing grace to do its work produced godliness and transformation.

Grace Empowers

Grace has a rhythm that is at odds with striving. It is so important to know where we are operating from. In the new covenant it is through faith that we have entered into a position of rest

Hebrews 4 v 9 to 10

So there remains a Sabbath rest for the people of God. For the one who has entered His rest has himself also rested from his works, as God did from His.

So much of religion is about seeking the approval of God through our efforts, striving and hard work. In the new covenant we live from the inside out, from a position of knowing we are loved and accepted in Christ.

Ephesians 1 v 5 to 6

having predestined us to adoption as sons by Jesus Christ to Himself, according to the good pleasure of His will, to the praise of the glory of His grace, by which He made us accepted in the Beloved.

Jesus has now provided a different way of living where we live in union with him. He invites us to a lifestyle of rest.

Matthew 11 v 28 to 30

Are you tired? Worn out? Burned out on religion? Come to me. Get away with me and you'll recover your life. I'll show you how to take a real rest. Walk with me and work with me—watch how I do it. Learn the unforced rhythms of grace. I won't lay anything heavy or ill-fitting on you. Keep company with me and you'll learn to live freely and lightly."

So does Grace mean laziness?

Paul the apostle is the man who brought much of the revelation of grace in the new covenant and yet is open about the abundance of his labours.

1 Corinthians 15 v 10

But by the grace of God I am what I am, and His grace toward me did not prove vain; but I laboured even more than all of them, yet not I, but the grace of God with me.

Grace is what made Paul who he was and he was conscious that it was grace that empowered him to do all the Lord had called him to. It is the miraculous secret of the new creation we read about in Galatians

Galatians 2 v 20

*have been crucified with Christ; and it is no longer I who live,
but Christ lives in me; and the life which I now live in the flesh I
live by faith in the Son of God, who loved me and gave Himself
up for me.*

Under grace we are still busy but it is a different kind of
busyness. It never forces us, drives us or places heavy burdens
on us but it works in us fulfilling his purpose.

Philippians 2 v 13

*for it is God who is at work in you, both to will and to work for
His good pleasure.*

It is a supernatural empowerment that sustains us even in the
most trying of circumstances. Look at the experience of Paul
and his testimony of God's grace.

2 Corinthians 11 v 23 to 28

*Are they servants of Christ?—I speak as if insane—I more so; in
far more labors, in far more imprisonments, beaten times
without number, often in danger of death. Five times I received
from the Jews thirty-nine lashes. Three times I was beaten with
rods, once I was stoned, three times I was shipwrecked, a night
and a day I have spent in the deep. I have been on frequent
journeys, in dangers from rivers, dangers from robbers,
dangers from my countrymen, dangers from the Gentiles,
dangers in the city, dangers in the wilderness, dangers on the
sea, dangers among false brethren; I have been in labor and
hardship, through many sleepless nights, in hunger and thirst,
often without food, in cold and exposure. Apart from such*

external things, there is the daily pressure on me of concern for all the churches.

2 Corinthians 12 v 9

And He has said to me, "My grace is sufficient for you, for power is perfected in weakness."

Grace is indomitable and all conquering! Our life is now hid with Christ in God and everything we are and receive in Christ is because of grace.

Ephesians 2 v 7

and He did this] so that in the ages to come He might [clearly] show the immeasurable and unsurpassed riches of His grace in [His] kindness toward us in Christ Jesus [by providing for our redemption].

We have a choice to make. Our decisions determine our destiny. We can try to do the work in our own strength or we can make grace work for us, in us and through us.

Curses and Blessings

The whole area of curses and blessings is a massive area in the church particularly those with a charismatic churchmanship. I have dealt with so many people who feel they are cursed in their lives because of sins they have committed sometimes decades ago. There is one chapter in the Bible which is a basis for a lot of this thinking and that is Deuteronomy 28. In summary the chapter outlines the blessings of obedience and the curses of disobedience. Remember the old covenant is based on the principle if you obey and behave you will be blessed. If ,however, you disobey you will be cursed. Curses outlined cover everything negative you could possibly encounter. It is important we renew our minds in this area by developing a new covenant mindset.

Jesus took our curse

The good news of the Gospel is that Jesus took our curse. Deuteronomy 28 now gets its correct context in the finished work of the cross.

Galatians 3 v 13

Christ redeemed us from the curse of the Law, having become a curse for us—for it is written, "Cursed is everyone who hangs on a tree

Everything that was written against us in the law has been removed. Praise God!

Colossians 2 v 14

having canceled out the certificate of debt consisting of decrees against us, which was hostile to us; and He has taken it out of the way, having nailed it to the cross.

Romans 7 v 6

But now we have been released from the Law, having died to that by which we were bound, so that we serve in newness of the Spirit and not in oldness of the letter.

If we are released from what is written in the law we are also released from its curse.

Blessing is your new position

Many times I have people come to me and asked me to bless them. It is always a joy to pray for people but the reality is that they couldn't be more blessed than what they are! You are blessed, you are blessed as you go out and you are blessed as you come in every part of your life is blessed.

Ephesians 1 v 3

Blessed be the God and Father of our Lord Jesus Christ, who has blessed us with every spiritual blessing in the heavenly places in Christ,

Every means every. Whatever blessing you think you need is already yours in Christ. By faith we reach into heaven and we bring it to the Earth. Also every blessing in the old he is now fulfilled in Christ and has become yours.

2 Corinthians 1 v 20

or as many as are the promises of God, in Him they are yes; therefore also through Him is our Amen to the glory of God through us.

When we approach a chapter like Deuteronomy 28 we take it through Jesus and the cross. The curse is broken and the promises have become ours.

Luke 6 v 28

bless those who curse you, pray for those who are abusive to you

What about generational curses?

A popular area of teaching is generational curses. This teaching is taken from the following verse

Exodus 34 v 7

yet He will by no means leave the guilty unpunished, visiting the iniquity of fathers on the children and on the grandchildren to the third and fourth generations.

Family traits, limitations and moral failures are seen as being the result of the sins that people have committed. It is believed that these sins
have opened the door for a family to be cursed. This is because the Lord is remembering the sins to the third and fourth generation.

What does the new covenant say about this?

Hebrews 8 v 12

"For I will be merciful to their iniquities,
And I will remember their sins no more."

Hebrews 10 v 17

"And their sins and their lawless deeds
I will remember no more."

The old covenant says God will not forget our sins but in the new covenant it says that he will remember our sins no more. Many people think when bad things happen this is God's punishment on them because of things they've done wrong. The thinking is often based around what happened to David when he committed adultery with Bathsheba and then arranged for Bathsheba's husband to be killed. In the story David's baby dies. We need to remember that David was in the old covenant but we are in the new covenant where the cross stands between the two covenants. We now live in the freedom of all that Jesus accomplished. We are totally loved, accepted and free from the fear of punishment.

1 John 4 v 18

There is no fear in love; but perfect love casts out fear, because fear involves punishment, and the one who fears is not perfected in love.

How do we speak?

I remember a few years ago being in a prayer meeting when suddenly people started praying about the Islamic world and particularly Dubai. They started to pray that the hotels would be destroyed and God's judgement will come on the city. I couldn't bring an amen to those prayers! Not only was the theology faulty but the heart attitude was poor . I did smile to myself as I really like Dubai and have enjoyed its hotels and know that there are many large churches in the city including one with a membership of 7000 people.

It highlighted to me something that is prevalent particularly in prophetic movements. I've heard people cursing communities, politicians, churches and church leaders. Sadly many times people have spoken curses over me so what does the new covenant tell us about such things.

Luke 6 v 28

bless those who curse you, pray for those who mistreat you.

James 3 v10

With it we bless our Lord and Father, and with it we curse men, who have been made in the likeness of God; from the same mouth come both blessing and cursing. My brethren, these things ought not to be this way.

Here the writer reminds us that we are to be those who use our mouth to bless people. Our words are to be used for the one purpose of blessing people and can bring life, joy, peace, healing and freedom to all.

Romans 12 v 14

Bless those who persecute you; bless and do not curse

This blessing even extends to our enemies and those who oppose us! We no longer use our words to judge and destroy others but instead we are motivated by love. Jesus spoke life and so do we.

John 6 v 63

It is the Spirit who gives life; the flesh profits nothing; the words that I have spoken to you are spirit and are life.

Words are incredibly powerful and in the new covenant it is clear both in the teachings of Jesus and in the apostolic letters that we use words to bless and build up others.

Outside or Inside

Another one of the big contrasts of the old covenant and the new covenant is whether we live from the outside or the inside. In the old covenant the emphasis was on living externally by rules and regulations. Also, our relationship with God was one where he was removed from us and to be found distant from us in heaven. He was what I will call ' the remote God '. This, however, changes in the new covenant where we now live from the inside, so let's see what this looks like in a few different areas

The kingdom

When we hold to a new covenant understanding we find that it will affect our thinking on many issues such as the church, the end times, and the kingdom.

What do we mean by the kingdom?

The simplest definition would be the Kings domain. It would be where we see the rule and reign of God. Under the old covenant that kingdom was external. When Jesus arrived on the scene his message was about that external coming kingdom.

Mark 1 v 14 &15

Now after John had been taken into custody, Jesus came into Galilee, preaching the gospel of God, and saying, "The time is fulfilled, and the kingdom of God is at hand; repent and believe in the gospel."

Here he is saying it's within reach.......almost here. Then as this gospel of the kingdom is declared Jesus makes an astonishing statement.

Luke 17 v 20 to 21

Now having been questioned by the Pharisees as to when the kingdom of God was coming, He answered them and said, "The kingdom of God is not coming with signs to be observed; nor will they say, 'Look, here it is!' or, 'There it is!' For behold, the kingdom of God is within you "

Jesus is speaking of a time when the kingdom will be within us. This again is the mystery of the new covenant when we will be in Christ and Christ will be in us. The king taking residence in each of our lives. So what does this look like in practical terms.

Romans 14 v17

for the kingdom of God is not eating and drinking, but righteousness and peace and joy in the Holy Spirit

The kingdom is no longer about externals i.e. what we eat or drink but it's about the internals of life in the Holy Spirit. Righteousness, peace and joy are now all resident within us.

This is the life transforming gospel. His kingdom is no longer within reach but it is now inside you with all the authority that was secured when Jesus died and rose again. This is the gospel we now preach not the covering of sin but the removal of all that put us into hiding from the father. Sin and the powers of darkness are defeated. This is the gospel of the kingdom.

Matthew 24 v 14

This gospel of the kingdom shall be preached in the whole world as a testimony to all the nations, and then the end will come

Many people are fascinated almost obsessed with the signs of the times but rarely reference this scripture when talking about Matthew 24. It is clear that the end is linked directly to the kingdoms advance in the nations. This is what is talked about in the book of Revelation.

Revelation 11 v 15

The kingdom of the world has become the kingdom of our Lord and of His Christ; and He will reign forever and ever."

The glory

If there is one area where the church often gets stuck between covenants it is with the glory of God.

Isaiah 64 v 1

*Oh, that You would rend the heavens and come down,
That the mountains might quake at Your presence*

Invariably people often quote this verse in prayer meetings but will quote it ' as your glory come down' . On one level that is perfectly fine because God and his glory are one. He is glory! When we look at this though in the light of the new covenant we realise that he has already come down this is what the incarnation is all about. When Jesus entered the world he came down with his glory.

John 1 v 14

And the Word became flesh, and dwelt among us, and we saw His glory, glory as of the only begotten from the Father, full of grace and truth.

Old covenant glory

In the old covenant we noticed that glory comes in a form. It might be a cloud like we see in the dedication of Solomon's temple. It may be a fire as we see in Moses encounter with God in the burning bush. In every instance it is something external. The other interesting thing to note is that in the old covenant the glory will come and go. Another old covenant term being used in church circles is the word Ichabod which means the glory has departed. We often hear people speaking about churches that have hit on hard times and someone will say ' ichabod is written over that church '. So let's have a look at glory in the new covenant.

New covenant glory

We have already noted earlier in this book that we are recipients of the very same glory that Jesus has, so where is this glory now found?

Colossians 1 v25-27

Of this church I was made a minister according to the stewardship from God bestowed on me for your benefit, so that I might fully carry out the preaching of the word of God, that is, the mystery which has been hidden from the past ages and generations, but has now been manifested to His saints, to whom God willed to make known what is the riches of the glory of this mystery among the Gentiles, which is Christ in you, the hope of glory

This glory is no longer fading and it no longer diminishes, it is actually an ever increasing glory

2 Corinthians 3v18

But we all, with unveiled face, beholding as in a mirror the glory of the Lord, are being transformed into the same image from glory to glory, just as from the Lord, the Spirit.

The assurance for us is that Ichabod no longer applies but we have been set up to experience ever increasing levels of glory. Everything about the Lord is about increase. In John 15 we read that he has designed us to bear fruit, more fruit, much fruit. We see again he is committed to our continual growth and our continual increase. That growth and increase is realised as we learn to live from the inside out.

The Spirit

Once again in the old covenant we see that the Holy Spirit came upon people whereas in the new covenant he flows out from people.

John 7 verse 37 to 39

Now on the last day, the great day of the feast, Jesus stood and cried out, saying, if anyone is thirsty, let him come to Me and drink. He who believes in Me, as the Scripture said, 'From his innermost being will flow rivers of living water.'" But this He spoke of the Spirit, whom those who believed in Him were to receive; for the Spirit was not yet given, because Jesus was not yet glorified.

Here Jesus is prophesying that after he is glorified that the Spirit will be poured out and received. This glorification we see in his ascension

Acts 1 verse 9

And after He had said these things, He was lifted up while they were looking on, and a cloud received Him out of their sight.

He is now risen, ascended and glorified and the Spirit has been poured out. The Holy Spirit now fills us and flows from us with life. The fruit of the spirit is now the natural consequence of him living inside us. Someone once said apple trees don't try to produce apples but it is natural for them to do so. As the apple sap flows through the tree so apples are produced. As the Holy Spirit from our spirit (inner man) flows into our mind, emotions and body so we think like him, talk like him and walk like him. Also, when he lives within us the gifts of the Spirit are distributed to us and we start to move in his power.

No more does the Spirit come and go but he is now resident within us. His gift and callings remain.

Romans 11 v 29

for the gifts and the calling of God are irrevocable

Sometimes people in the church get perplexed as to why God's power can be seen flowing through people even when there is evidence of sin in their lives. I knew of one Christian leader who had a powerful ministry where he was going to shopping centres and seeing incredible healings take place including people being hauled out of wheelchairs. All the time he was doing this he remained in an adulterous relationship. Many people were perplexed but it was a reminder that the Holy

Spirits gifts are gifts and not loans. This is why I often advise people not to follow a persons gift but instead follow their character. Grace is the lavish liberal giving of gifts from a father who loves us.

Live from the inside

The new covenant is full of revelation about living from the inside.

Romans 8 v 11

But if the Spirit of Him who raised Jesus from the dead dwells in you, He who raised Christ Jesus from the dead will also give life to your mortal bodies through His Spirit who dwells in you.

This verse reminds us that the very same resurrection life that Jesus carries is now at work from the inside of us.

I remember one evening we were doing a healing meeting in our hometown of Bolton. It was a powerful time with many people saved and healed. We were also seeing a lot of people fall on the floor when we touched them, this is what charismatics term being slain in the Spirit. As all of this was happening a group of young people came into the meeting and started having fun by mimicking what was happening. One of the group would lay hands on his friend and that friend would throw himself on the floor. It was hilarious to watch! After a few minutes they were called forward giggling all the time like young people do. I asked one of them to stand maybe a couple of metres away from me and then from my inner man I released the Holy Spirit. Without any hands laid on them this young person fell on the floor. It was amazing to see the shock on the faces of these youngsters. Suddenly, they realised that Jesus is alive and real.

Paul the apostle in his letter to the church at Ephesus said the following

Ephesians 3 v 20 to 21

Now to Him who is able to do far more abundantly beyond all that we ask or think, according to the power that works within us, to Him be the glory in the church and in Christ Jesus to all generations forever and ever. Amen.

Often when we think of his ability we think outside ourselves, however, the incredible mind blowing things he is able to do are inside us waiting to come out. Verse 20 reminds us that it is according to the power that works within us. In the better new covenant the answers are not on the outside but they are now within us.

Man of God or People of God

One of the more evident differences between the old and the new covenant is the role of ministers/leaders. I remember a number of years ago receiving an SMS off someone where they referred to me as MOG I must submit it gave me a lot of amusement because in the UK a MOG is a cat. Obviously they were referring to me as a man of God and often as I travel around people will greet me in such a manner, there is truth in this I am a man of God but no more so than other men within the body of Christ. In the old covenant the minister would have an elevated position. As a priest or a prophet he would stand between God and the people of God. He would enquire of the Lord and instruct people what the Lord wanted. In the priesthood that would be by the following of written ordinances and in the role of the prophet it was a revelation of God's way. There was a very real sense in which the people were totally dependent on their leaders with no means other than the prophet to know the voice of God.

Jesus the difference

Right at the heart of this book the message I'm wanting to convey is that Jesus makes the difference. He is now the mediator!

1 Timothy 2 v 5

For there is one God, and one mediator also between God and men, the man Christ Jesus,

The one who stands before you and the Father is Jesus. In salvation he is the way to the father although Jesus is more than a go-between (a Mr fixer) but he enables us to know the Father and the Fathers love for ourselves. As a good Shepherd who laid down his life for the sheep he enables us to know the voice of God for ourselves.

John 10 v 27

My sheep hear My voice, and I know them,

There is no need now to run around looking for a prophet who will tell us what to do but we can go direct to the Father who is longing to speak into our lives. He has more thoughts about us than we can fully comprehend!

In the old covenant there was an elite who were closer to God, but at the cross every barrier was broken including the clergy/laity Barrier. Jesus is a prophet , priest and king who is growing a kingdom of prophets, priests and kings. Under the old we were excluded but in the new covenant we are now included

1 Peter 2 v 9

But you are a chosen race, a royal priesthood, a holy nation, a people for God's own possession, so that you may proclaim the excellencies of Him who has called you out of darkness into His marvelous light;

Revelation 1 v 6

and He has made us to be a kingdom, priests to His God and Father—to Him be the glory and the dominion forever and ever. Amen.

Revelation 5 v 10

You have made them to be a kingdom and priests to our God; and they will reign upon the earth

This is who we are now it is part of our identity. We are royalty so dignity, worth and value are found in us. We are truly regal.

Kings

Kings reign over everything in their territory. I often talk about the lion being the king of its territory. If the lion roars everything around it trembles. We have a roar inside us because we are kings with authority. When we roar the enemy trembles. We are rulers and we reign in life.

Romans 5 v 17

For if by the transgression of the one, death reigned through the one, much more those who receive the abundance of grace and of the gift of righteousness will reign in life through the One, Jesus Christ.

We now bring the jurisdiction of heaven to earth. As glorious new creations we now reign in life by Jesus Christ. A number of years ago I was privileged to visit Chile. One town we visited was called Curanilahue it was a town of around 33,000 people and had been suffering greatly with men committing suicide after the local coal mines were forced to shutdown. The churches in the town decided that they would pray every week for a reduction in the suicide rate. After nine months the suicide rate had drastically reduced and the churches started to pray that new businesses and prosperity would come to the town. Shortly after praying for this the Chilean government started to divert funding to Curanilahue and the town started to prosper again. When we were there around 45% of the population were born again. There were 120 churches in the small town and around 60 of those churches worked very closely together. There also was such an incredible sense of peace over the place. There was a group of 200 witches from around the world who heard about what God was doing and decided they would visit the town to stop God's work through their witchcraft. When they arrived the church responded by walking round the streets claiming the town for Jesus. After two weeks every witch had left town as they said they had no power to do anything . This is the very real and incredible authority the church has when we start operating as kings.

Priest

As priests we are bringing a continual offering before the Lord. This often starts with the presenting of our lives

Romans 12 v 1-2

Therefore I urge you, brethren, by the mercies of God, to present your bodies a living and holy sacrifice, acceptable to God, which is your spiritual service of worship. And do not be conformed to this world, but be transformed by the renewing of your mind, so that you may prove what the will of God is, that which is good and acceptable and perfect.

It also involves our offering of worship

Hebrews 13 v 15

Through Him then, let us continually offer up a sacrifice of praise to God, that is, the fruit of lips that give thanks to His name

And our giving of time, money and love is part of our priestly ministry.

Hebrews 13 v 16

And do not neglect doing good and sharing, for with such sacrifices God is pleased.

And our Prayer for all men.

1 Timothy 2 verse 1 - 4

First of all, then, I urge that entreaties and prayers, petitions and thanksgivings, be made on behalf of all men, for kings and all who are in authority, so that we may lead a tranquil and quiet life in all godliness and dignity. This is good and acceptable in the sight of God our Savior, who desires all men to be saved and to come to the knowledge of the truth

Prophets

Now we can all hear the voice of God and move in prophecy. This was the longing of Paul the apostle when he wrote to the highly charismatic church in Corinth.

1 Corinthians 14 v 5

Now I wish that you all spoke in tongues, but even more that you would prophesy; and greater is one who prophesies than one who speaks in tongues, unless he interprets, so that the church may receive edifying.

Within us now is the spirit of prophecy which speaks of Jesus.

Revelation 19 v 10

Then I fell at his feet to worship him. But he *said to me, "Do not do that; I am a fellow servant of yours and your brethren

who hold the testimony of Jesus; worship God. For the
testimony of Jesus is the spirit of prophecy."

Leadership in the new covenant

So if we acknowledge that Jesus has broken the clergy/laity barrier and all can know God for themselves and minister in the power of the spirit does this mean there is no need for leadership in the church?

Ephesians 4 v 11 - 16

And He gave some as apostles, and some as prophets, and some as evangelists, and some as pastors and teachers, for the equipping of the saints for the work of service, to the building up of the body of Christ; until we all attain to the unity of the faith, and of the knowledge of the Son of God, to a mature man, to the measure of the stature which belongs to the fullness of Christ. As a result, we are no longer to be children, tossed here and there by waves and carried about by every wind of doctrine, by the trickery of men, by craftiness in deceitful scheming; but speaking the truth in love, we are to grow up in all aspects into Him who is the head, even Christ, from whom the whole body, being fitted and held together by what every joint supplies, according to the proper working of each individual part, causes the growth of the body for the building up of itself in love.

There is still leadership in the new covenant but it no longer works as an intermediary but instead grows, equips and releases people in ministry. What is the function of this leadership? In Ephesians four verse 12 and 13 we see that leadership does 3 things

1) Equips people for works for service

No longer is all the work done by a few but it is now done by the many. When Jesus returned to the Father he said it was expedient. This simply means more efficient. Why ? Because he could pour out the Holy Spirit and see his life reproduced in the sons of men. We went from one son of God to many. One has multiplied into millions through the finished work of the cross.

2) Produces unity

Unity is an expression of God's heart. Jesus died to form one new man. It was the prayer that Jesus prayed in John 17. One of the reasons we are passionate about the trinity is because it reveals the relational nature of the Godhead. A perfect unity of mutual honouring and submission. The Church too is built on relationships of mutual honouring and submission. It starts with leadership as all Godly ministry will endeavour to maintain unity in the body of Christ.

John 17 v 20-21

"I do not ask on behalf of these alone, but for those also who believe in Me through their word; that they may all be one; even as You, Father, are in Me and I in You, that they also may be in Us, so that the world may believe that You sent Me.

3) Helps people know Jesus

All ministry is now geared up to producing a dependency on Jesus. Its goal is for people to know him and to recognise his voice and become conformed to his likeness. The Apostolic cry is found in Galatians 4v19.

Galatians 4 v 19

My children, with whom I am again in labor until Christ is formed in you

Family model

Church isn't an organisation built on business principles but it is a living organism where healthy relationships are at its core. The Church is now built on a family model where those in leadership are Fathers and mothers to those they care for. In natural parenting there are different seasons and phases of life. When young the children are dependent on their parents but as they grow the parents help them mature so they are able to take on responsibility. They then leave home and establish their own households where they become fathers and mothers in their own right. This is the cycle of life, a natural progression. In the Church it is exactly the same, there are the same steps, development and progression.

Where is the Temple?

In the old covenant so much of the worship of God centred around a physical dwelling mainly the tabernacle and then the temple. We've already seen that the new covenant was fully instituted when the temple was destroyed in A.D. 70.

A new covenant concept of tabernacle and temple

It is amazing how much of our focus today still centres around buildings. We find ourselves often slipping in to phrases like ' going to church ' or welcome to the ' house of the Lord'. But what do we see in the context of the new covenant.

His people are his temple

In the old covenant the glory of the Lord would fill the temple. We saw this in the dedication of the temple where the glory cloud came in and the priests were unable to minister. In the new covenant his glory now resides in people and his temple is our individual life.

1 Corinthians 6 v 19

Or do you not know that your body is a temple of the Holy Spirit who is in you, whom you have from God, and that you are not your own?

We also see that there is a corporate dimension to this temple

Ephesians 2 v 19 to 21

So then you are no longer strangers and aliens, but you are fellow citizens with the saints, and are of God's household, having been built on the foundation of the apostles and prophets, Christ Jesus Himself being the corner stone, in whom the whole building, being fitted together, is growing into a holy temple in the Lord, in whom you also are being built together into a dwelling of God in the Spirit.

This temple is held together by Christ the cornerstone and it's established on apostolic mission and prophetic revelation. This is further reinforced in the famous verses

1 Peter 2 v 9

But you are a chosen race, a royal priesthood, a holy nation, a people for God's own possession, so that you may proclaim the

excellencies of Him who has called you out of darkness into His marvelous light;

Here Peter reminds us of God's heart to have a priesthood of people and a nation belonging to him. All of these are now expressed through the living stones of the church where we have been brought together relationally. I often say we are chiselled and wedged together. We are now a spiritual house where he lives!

Revelation 21 v 3

And I heard a loud voice from the throne, saying, "Behold, the tabernacle of God is among men, and He will dwell among them, and they shall be His people, and God Himself will be among them

We are now his dwelling place (tabernacle). He has come to stay and not leave. No more visitations because we are now his habitation!

David's tent

When King David brought the ark of God's presence back to Jerusalem he set up a special tent of worship in the middle of the city.

1 Chronicles 16v1

And they brought in the ark of God and placed it inside the tent which David had pitched for it, and they offered burnt offerings and peace offerings before God.

David recognised that God was worthy of extravagant worship and that his presence was worth celebrating. David's tabernacle hosted over 30 years of day and night worship that was open for the people to come and worship in God's presence without the separation of the veil. There were no barriers to people entering! This is a prophetic picture of the new covenant where Jesus made a way for us on the cross - a people re-united with God pouring out their hearts in response to his love. The Apostle James addressed the council at Jerusalem with the Amos 9 prophecy about the ' restoration of David's fallen tent '.

Acts 15 v 13 to 18

After they had stopped speaking, James answered, saying, "Brethren, listen to me. Simeon has related how God first concerned Himself about taking from among the Gentiles a people for His name. With this the words of the Prophets agree, just as it is written,
'After these things I will return,
And I will rebuild the tabernacle of David which has fallen,
And I will rebuild its ruins,
And I will restore it,
So that the rest of mankind may seek the Lord,
And all the Gentiles who are called by My name,'
Says the Lord, who makes these things known from long ago.

Once again everyone can participate in David's tent. This is the place of the abiding presence of the Lord and of continual worship. It is a place of intimacy and the astounding thing is we are now David's tent. Now his presence is within us and the offering of our lives to him and his cause is our worship.

Romans12v1

Therefore I urge you, brethren, by the mercies of God, to present your bodies a living and holy sacrifice, acceptable to God, which is your spiritual service of worship

Portals

Linked to this whole idea of buildings holding a special presence is the concept of portals. This is taken from Jacobs encounter with the Lord when he sees a ladder with angels ascending and descending. He goes on to call the place a gateway to heaven.

Genesis 28 v 10 to 17

Then Jacob departed from Beersheba and went toward Haran. He came to a certain place and spent the night there, because the sun had set; and he took one of the stones of the place and put it under his head, and lay down in that place. He had a dream, and behold, a ladder was set on the earth with its top reaching to heaven; and behold, the angels of God were ascending and descending on it. And behold, the Lord stood above it and said, "I am the Lord, the God of your father Abraham and the God of Isaac; the land on which you lie, I will give it to you and to your descendants. Your descendants will also be like the dust of the earth, and you will spread out to the west and to the east and to the north and to the south; and in you and in your descendants shall all the families of the earth be blessed. Behold, I am with you and will keep you wherever you go, and will bring you back to this land; for I will not leave you until I have done what I have promised you." Then Jacob awoke from his sleep and said, "Surely the Lord is in this place, and I did not know it." He was afraid and said, "How awesome is this place! This is none other than the house of God, and this is the gate of heaven."

When Jesus walked on the earth he declared that he was now that ladder with angels ascending and descending. He is a gateway place where Heaven invades the earth.

John 1 v 51

And He said to him, "Truly, truly, I say to you, you will see the heavens opened and the angels of God ascending and descending on the Son of Man."

The amazing truth is that we too are now a portal, gateway and ladder bringing heaven to earth. Why ? Because we are now like Jesus!

1 John 4 v 17

By this, love is perfected with us, so that we may have confidence in the day of judgment; because as He is, so also are we in this world.

When we walk in places the atmosphere changes! Heaviness gives way to lightness. We can walk into dark places and the darkness has to flee because the light has been switched on. This is the victory of the Gospel!

John 1 v 5

The Light shines in the darkness, and the darkness did not comprehend it.

When the truth of this settles in our spirit it transforms us. His presence within us can break out of us at any time making any place Holy! Why? Because he is there in us.

In the old covenant we see that there were many barriers. These included man and God, slaves and free people, Jews and Gentiles, men and women. When Jesus died every barrier was broken and oneness became possible. Jesus destroyed the apparent separation and exclusion that was experienced by many.

Ephesians 2 v14 -16

For he himself is our peace, who has made the two groups one and has destroyed the barrier, the dividing wall of hostility, by setting aside in his flesh the law with its commands and regulations. His purpose was to create in himself one new humanity out of the two, thus making peace, and in one body to reconcile both of them to God through the cross, by which he put to death their hostility.

This is totally comprehensive! It is absolute, the enmity/barrier has been abolished.

So how do things look in the new covenant

Galatians 3 v 28

There is neither Jew nor Gentile, neither slave nor free, nor is there male and female, for you are all one in Christ Jesus.

Here Paul in his letter to the church at Galatia describes what barriers have been broken down. Just a little reflection reveals to us what a radical statement this is. For some there is so much to lose and for others there is so much to gain. Paul Cain once said God offends the mind to reveal the heart and here we can see the apparent offences! The Greeks take offence because they consider their culture and intellect superior to others. The Romans are offended because they have many slaves in their household who they consider inferior. Then the men are upset because they lose their control over the women. If that isn't enough the Jews are offended because in Paul's statement they're no longer more special than the Gentiles. All of this is the fulfilment of the Ministry of Jesus.

Luke 12 v 49

I've come to start a fire on this earth—how I wish it were blazing right now! I've come to change everything, turn everything rightside up—how I long for it to be finished!

It is the upside down kingdom at work where hierarchy is done away with and one new man is formed in Christ. What a gospel we have that goes right to the very heart of things and sows the seeds of a love revolution.

Sadly we still sometimes see these barriers in place, so let's have a look at the biblical basis for their removal.

Jews or Gentiles

If there is one subject that has caused great controversy over the years it is most likely the subject of Israel and the Jewish people. All would agree that in the old covenant Gods purposes centred around the nation of Israel. They were his special chosen people, however, it is in the new covenant we see a divergence of understanding.

Search for a nation

Gods heart has always been for a people/nation. At the beginning of time we see this in his relationship with Adam, where mans original intent is to be a glory carrier, however, due to the fall and mans pride and conceit the tower of Babel sees nations being formed. He then sets aside a nation Israel who will be set apart from other nations with a call to carry his glory. This is until Jesus comes to the Earth as the second Adam conquering sin and paving the way for a new nation made up of both jew and gentile to carry his glory. The church is now that special chosen people.

1 Peter 2 v 9

But you are a chosen race, a royal priesthood, a holy nation, a people for God's own possession, so that you may proclaim the excellencies of Him who has called you out of darkness into His marvelous light;

We are glory carriers. Gods original intent was that mankind would reveal Gods heart and nature. A father in love with his family. Now the church fulfils this mission.

One new man

Ephesians 2 v 11-19

Therefore remember that formerly you, the Gentiles in the flesh, who are called
"Uncircumcision" by the so-called "Circumcision," which is performed in the flesh by human hands remember that you were at that time separate from Christ, excluded from the commonwealth of Israel, and strangers to the covenants of promise, having no hope and without God in the world. But now in Christ Jesus you who formerly were far off have been brought near by the blood of Christ. For He Himself is our peace, who made both groups into one and broke down the barrier of the dividing wall, by abolishing in His flesh the

enmity, which is the Law of commandments contained in ordinances, so that in Himself He might make the two into one new man, thus establishing peace, and might reconcile them both in one body to God through the cross, by it having put to death the enmity. And He came and preached peace to you who were far away, and peace to those who were near; for through Him we both have our access in one Spirit to the Father. So then you are no longer strangers and aliens, but you are fellow citizens with the saints, and are of God's household

What a powerful scripture this is! There was a time when as Gentiles we were excluded looking from the outside in. The covenants weren't ours and the promises weren't ours also..........until Jesus! When he died the written code, the law and the separation was done away with and one new man was formed. There are no special people and then extra special people. In verse 18 it tells us 'we both' that is Jews and Gentiles through Jesus have access to the father by the holy spirit

A heart for all people

When I have shared this message in the past there have been those that accuse me of anti-Semitism. Let me be clear I love Jewish people and the nation of Israel. As a ministry we have supported those who have gone to Israel preaching the gospel. We do, however, love all people equally that is Jew, Arab and every other gentle nation. We now rejoice when people receive salvation and become part of the one new man.

An appeal for Graciousness

Whilst touching on this controversial subject I want to encourage people to not go to war with others over the issue of Israel. We can hold our convictions and still honour those with different convictions. I have good friends with a different perspective on the nation of Israel and a different view of the end times but I can still see Jesus in them. This is maybe what Paul was talking about when he encouraged the church at Corinth to no longer recognise people according to the flesh. Let's rejoice that the barriers have gone and let's live together peacefully as the one new man.

Male or female

There is often been a lot of controversy around Paul's views and opinions of women. We do, however, see that women played an important part in the life of the early Church and were significant in the apostolic ministry of Paul. In his letters he refers to at least 17 women who worked closely with him. The context of Galatians 3 v 28 is that all are included in Christ irrespective of gender and background. We do see that in the new covenant the barriers are broken down and in the life of both Jesus and Paul women played an importantly vital role.

Phoebe is referred to in Romans 16 and in all the translations there is no doubt about the esteem that Paul holds her in. In most translations she is referred to as a ' helper to many, including myself '. The word translated helper is the word Prostasis which is more accurately translated as leader. This makes this passage revolutionary. Paul is saying a ' woman ' is a leader to many and a leader to him.

Romans 16 v 2

Now, let me introduce to you our dear and beloved sister in the faith, Phoebe, a shining minister of the church in Cenchrea. I am sending her with this letter and ask that you shower her with your hospitality when she arrives. Embrace her with honor, as is fitting for one who belongs to the Lord and is set apart for him. I am entrusting her to you, so provide her whatever she may need, for she's been a great leader and champion for many—I know, for she's been that for even me!

Much of the early Church was gathered in homes and we see that the leaders of these Church's were sometimes women. Priscilla, Nympha, Mary, Lydia are all mentioned and the churches that met in their homes. Priscilla is also mentioned along with her husband equally as being instrumental in the growth and development of Apollos who himself exercised a significant apostolic ministry.

Acts 18 v 24-26

Now a Jew named Apollos, an Alexandrian by birth, an eloquent man, came to Ephesus; and he was mighty in the Scriptures. This man had been instructed in the way of the Lord; and being fervent in spirit, he was speaking and teaching accurately the things concerning Jesus, being acquainted only with the baptism of John; and he began to speak out boldly in the synagogue. But when Priscilla and Aquila heard him, they took him aside and explained to him the way of God more accurately

It is interesting that on four occasions Priscilla's name precedes that of her husband indicating the extent of her own influence and the esteem by which she is held.

Paul also refers to Euodia and Syntyche as co-workers. They are considered as those who worked alongside him and not for him. He acknowledges the full extent of their sacrifice and commitment.

The word struggle that is mentioned is the interpretation of a Greek word that would normally convey the idea of straining everything to attain a goal.

He then makes a startling statement referring to junia as not only having an apostolic ministry but being significant among the other predominantly male apostles.

Romans 16 v 7

Greet Andronicus and Junia, my kinsfolk and my fellow prisoners, who are outstanding in the view of the apostles, who also were in Christ before me.

In all of this it is clear to see that women were honoured, respected and included in their own right in the apostolic mission that Paul led. It is important that we don't pick out individual scriptures to develop a doctrinal stance. There are possibly 2 passages that appear to potentially contradict the above, however, the general revelation is of women having equal worth and value in the new covenant.

What about the controversial verses ?

The most controversial passage is the following

1 Timothy 2 v 9-15

Likewise, I want women to adorn themselves with proper clothing, modestly and discreetly, not with braided hair and gold or pearls or expensive apparel, but rather by means of good works, as is proper for women making a claim to godliness. A woman must quietly receive instruction with entire submissiveness. But I do not allow a woman to teach or to exercise authority over a man, but to remain quiet. For it was

Adam who was first created, and then Eve. And it was not Adam who was deceived, but the woman was deceived and became a wrongdoer. But women will be preserved through childbirth —if they continue in faith, love, and sanctity, with moderation.

The key to these Scriptures is understanding the context in which they were written. Paul had left Timothy to bring correction to the two prevalent teachings in Ephesians society that had started to infiltrate the church. The first was the teaching of the Artemis cult who believed that The worship of the goddess Artemis would bring women safety in childbirth. The second teaching was that of the Gnostics who believed you were saved through secret knowledge. They saw Eve as an example of the pursuit of knowledge through her act of eating of the tree of the knowledge of good and evil.
In 1 Timothy 2 v 9-15 Paul is addressing this false teaching.

What does he say ?

1) A woman should learn (1 Timothy 2v11)

Rather than undervalue women he is actually encouraging them to be active in learning thereby growing and developing and her understanding. This was incredibly countercultural in the society in which Paul lived where women were expected to remain uneducated.

2) A women should be silent and submissive (1 Timothy 2v11)

The word silent is the word Hesuchia which means to be calm and still. He is encouraging them to be open and receptive which are the hallmarks of good learners. At no point is he saying that they shouldn't talk.

3) A woman should not teach or have authority over a man (1 Timothy 2 v12)

The scripture has to be balanced against many others where Paul is actively encouraging women to teach. Remember the context for this passage is correcting false teaching against cults that were largely centred around women. It is an exhortation to a specific group of women at a specific time for a specific reason.

In this verse the command to not exercise of authority over a man is the word authentein which carries the notion of excessive domination. This is what Paul refers to not the Greek word exusia which is legitimate servant hearted authority.

4) The woman was deceived and sinned (1 Timothy 2 v 14)

This is a direct correction of the Gnostic belief that Eve was to be honoured for eating of the tree of the knowledge of good and evil. Paul makes it clear by reminding them that this was actually sin and rebellion.

Slave or free

Cultural barriers have gone, gender barriers have gone and now Paul emphasises that the economic barriers have gone. There could be no more powerful oppression than that of slavery which was commonplace in the time that Paul was writing. The dominant viewpoint was that slaves were less than human but in this one simple statement Paul reminds us that the gospel is about the infinite worth and value of every person. There is no more hierarchy and division in the Kingdom of God, no wonder this gospel was received and embraced with great joy by some and resisted with great force by others.

The Kingdom of God has always been a Kingdom of justice and righteousness.

Psalm 89 v 14

Righteousness and justice are the foundation of your throne; love and faithfulness go before you.

Isaiah 9 v 7

There will be no end to the increase of His government or of peace, On the throne of David and over his kingdom, To establish it and to uphold it with justice and righteousness From then on and forevermore. The zeal of the Lord of hosts will accomplish this.

There is no racial superiority, gender inequality or oppression of the powerless in the gospel. This is as much a part of the Kingdom manifesto as signs, wonders and miracles. When Jesus taught us to pray ' Your Kingdom come, your will be done ' this is what it looks like. There is now a beautiful mystical union with Christ and with each other. When Jesus meets the women at the Well he breaks all the barriers. He is speaking with a woman, a non Jew and a person of poor social standing and yet he ministers love, compassion and restoration into her life. The better Covenant breaks the barriers and gives equal access to all.

This new and better way is summed up greatly in the lyrics of Godfrey Birtills song ' When I look at the blood '

When I look at the blood
All I see is love love love
When I stop at the cross
I can see the love of God

But I can't see competition
I can't see hierarchy
I can't see pride or prejudice
Or the abuse of authority
I can't see lust for power
I can't see manipulation
I can't see rage or anger or selfish ambition

When I look at the blood
All I see is love love love
When I stop at the cross
I can see the love of God

But I can't see unforgiveness
I can't see hate or envy
I can't see stupid fighting;
Or bitterness or jealousy
I can't see empire building
I can't see self-importance
I can't see back stabbing or vanity
Or arrogance

When I look at the blood
All I see is love love love
When I stop at the cross
I can see the love of God

And I see surrender sacrifice
Salvation humility
Righteousness faithfulness
Grace forgiveness

Love love love
Love love love

New covenant law

Everything has changed we are now living in a new kingdom with a new government established on a new covenant. The old covenant was founded on the law of Moses whereas the new covenant is founded on the law of Christ! We are now living under that law

Galatians 6 v 2

Bear one another's burdens, and thereby fulfill the law of Christ.

1 Corinthians 9 v 21

to those who are without law, as without law, though not being without the law of God but under the law of Christ, so that I might win those who are without law.

What is the law of Christ?

We now understand that when Jesus walked the earth he started to introduce the idea of a different way and a new covenant. When the covenant was cut (the cross) and established(AD70) the understanding of what was involved in the new covenant started to grow. Jesus starts to introduce a new command (law)

John 13 v 34

new commandment I give to you, that you love one another, even as I have loved you, that you also love one another.

Jesus is introducing a new way of living as previously under the law the expectation was to love others like you love yourself. Now in a new covenant it is to love others like he loves us. We now love with unconditional love because we love like he loves and we have within us divine love waiting to be expressed. A few years ago I remember attending a church function where the local mayor was also in attendance. I was asked to speak for 10 minutes on relationships where I explained that we love with an unconditional love. The mayor subsequently got up and said only God can love with an unconditional love. It highlighted the contrast between the old covenant and new covenant mentality.

Romans 5 v 5

because the love of God has been poured out within our hearts through the Holy Spirit who was given to us.

The very same love that he has we now have because of the Holy Spirit residing in us.

What does his love look like?

It is loving all people equally.

The moment we say that we can think of people who have become our enemies but Jesus even covers this in the sermon on the mount.

Matthew 5 v 44

But I say to you, love your enemies and pray for those who persecute you,

It is unconditional

In the story of the prodigal there are no conditions laid down for the wandering son when he returns home. All we see is that the father wants him home!

It is sacrificial

This isn't the sacrifice of duty but of devotion.

1 John 3 v 16

We know love by this, that He laid down His life for us; and we ought to lay down our lives for the brethren

Once again this is how we love others by deferring to one another. The new covenant is about community. The law of the new covenant is demonstrated through the many commands that refer to our treatment of one another.

Raising the standard

Paul in his letter to the church at Corinth is bringing correction to excesses where people had forgotten the importance of love. Instead, sadly there was widespread selfishness being peddled under the banner of freedom. He devotes an important part of his letter to remind people of the divine standard of love

1 Corinthians 13 v 1 to 8

Love is patient, love is kind. It does not envy, it does not boast, it is not proud. It does not dishonor others, it is not self-seeking, it is not easily angered, it keeps no record of wrongs. Love does not delight in evil but rejoices with the

truth. It always protects, always trusts, always hopes, always perseveres. Love never fails.

Wow! This is the call to raise the bar. This is how we love because this is how he loves. This is the divine nature that we have received that lives inside us.

Love is patient

Love doesn't force the issue. It's not pushy but is willing to wait. It doesn't live for short-term gain but is willing to play the long game!

Love is kind

There is such a need for kindness in our world. I believe it is an underrated attribute. The dictionary says kindness is being friendly generous and considerate. That is who we are!

Love doesn't envy

Love is delighted when others succeed and experience favour because it understands generosity of spirit is a Kingdom hallmark.

Love doesn't boast and isn't proud

Everything we are and have is because of grace. This is why we boast in the finished work of Jesus. True humility isn't self abasement but is the recognition of our source and our openness to others.

Love doesn't dishonour

We don't honour people primarily for what they do or don't do but instead for who they are. People made in the image of God. We speak well of others and are gracious towards them. Honour is key to creating a supernatural environment.

Love isn't self seeking

A friend of mine once talked about the unholy trinity .... me, myself and I. Love isn't filled with selfish ambition even when choosing that way proves to be costly.

Love isn't easily angered

The key to responding out of love is understanding. Often when we consider others it takes the angst out of our emotions.

Love keeps no record of wrongs

This is a big one! Love doesn't remind someone of what they said or did in the past. To forgive is truly to forget.

Love delights in truth

Love doesn't live in the evil place of gossip, intrigue and conspiracy but rejoices when the true identity of God and his children is revealed.

Love always protects

Love doesn't expose others but seeks to protect. It covers a multitude of sins. This is a massive area of difference in old covenant and new covenant concepts. The old exposes whereas the new covers and protects.

Love always believe and hopes

Where trust has been broken, love heals, restores and once again trusts. Love is always hopeful of better times to come.

Love always perseveres

Love never gives up. The Lord hasn't given up on us and we don't give up on each other.

Love never fails

Love is eternal. It doesn't fade away. It always works everything for good.

This is the love that we now have in the new covenant. It is how we love and it is a fuller and better expression of love than what was experienced in the old covenant.

Forgiveness the foundation of love

We see that the fathers forgiveness is how we know we are loved. It is also vital in our relationships with one another. Sadly, relationships go wrong and people get hurt. Our response is often one of retreating and protecting ourselves from getting hurt again. The new covenant way though is the way of forgiveness

Ephesians 4 v 31 to 32

Get rid of all bitterness, rage and anger, brawling and slander, along with every form of malice. Be kind and compassionate

to one another, forgiving each other, just as in Christ God forgave you.

The new covenant law is very clear about what we do with our attitudes when they don't lineup with gods love. There are three crucial stages in the process of forgiveness

1) forgive

This is a decision, an act of the will. When I forgive others I also ask the Lord to heal me of the hurts and wounds that I have experienced. Our forgiveness is total and has no conditions attached to it.

2) bless

Jesus told us to bless our enemies because blessing is not a statement concerning a persons behaviour but instead reveals the heart and nature of God. Again, unconditionally we speak blessings into peoples lives.

3) release

We release people completely. We keep no record of wrongs committed.

When we do these three things it also opens up the way for a reconciliation and restoration.

This I believe fulfils the law of Christ. Many times when I've been mistreated I've heard the Holy spirit remind me that he loves my enemy as much as he loves me. That always puts an end to any argument. Let's release and demonstrate the new covenant and see the fathers love manifested in peoples lives.

New Covenant in a Nutshell

The following was seen on Facebook and sums up the better Covenant perfectly.

It is finished. The days of Elijah are finished as Jesus perfectly fulfils the Old Covenant and sheds His blood introducing and birthing the new Covenant between God and man.

You are now forbidden by the dying gasp of your Lord and Saviour from doing anything to obtain His blessings. Now, because of His work on the cross, they are freely available to whoever believes in what He did.

This is the only death that redefined history, crushed the head of satan, opened the doors of freedom to all who were oppressed, exchanged our filthy rags of righteousness with His glorious robes of righteousness, brings peace to all of us, bears our sicknesses and brings us complete healing, endured poverty to bring us riches, and embraced the shame of a traitor's execution to lift us from shame and enable us to sit freely on the most honoured throne in all of heaven and earth. Striving to impress God is finished, the tyranny of death is finished, the subjugation of humanity by satan is finished, the need for someone to stand in the gap is finished, the Fathers quest for an intercessor is finished, the message of salvation is now no longer just available to prophets seeing the future but the paymemt to give us access to the Father is finished, turning the good hope of the future into good news.

Now because of what Christ has done fear is finished, doubt is finished, hopelessness is finished, loneliness is finished, rejection is finished, sin is finished, the Curse is finished.

All religious rituals, praying in a certain place, at a certain mountain, at a certain time, with this offering or that sacrifice is finished. The way to Him is open and we can now worship in spirit and in truth

The need to find a priest to accept our offering is finished. He is now both our perfect priest and perfect offering.
The need to find a man of God to anoint us is finished. He is now our perfect Anointer and we have an anointing from Him

The need to clean ourselves up is finished. We are now clean.

The need to wait for the Spirit to descend is finished. The Spirit is now with us and if we believe and receive will be in us.

All punishment is finished. The punishment that brought us peace is on Him, so God will never punish the same sin twice and all sins were fully punished in Christ.

The need to venerate or imitate the Jewish religion is finished, and now the Jews and Gentiles are one church in Him, those near and those far are one through His blood

In Greek, it is finished is just one word, tetelestai. It means perfectly perfected or completely completed. Or perfectly completed, or completely perfected. The Old is now obsolete, the new has come.

Your old nature is finished. You, if you believe in this complete work are finished. You are crucified in Christ, and the life you now live by the faith of the Son of God.

Finally, the days of Jesus being the one and only Son of God are finished. Now through the cross, Jesus has brought many sons to glory! Glory to God it is finished!

Postscript - Contrast of Covenant

Old Covenant	New Covenant
The Letter	The Spirit
Kills.	Gives Life
Glory fades.	Glory increases
Condemnation	Righteousness
Passing away	Remains
Glorious	More Glorious

Law and Grace

Law

1. Reveals mans inability to keep the law

2. Given by Moses

3. Keeps us from coming to God

4. Condemns the sinner

5. Shuts every mouth

Grace

1. Man becomes a partaker of the Divine nature

2. Grace and truth by Jesus Christ

3. Invites us to come to God

4. Redeems the sinner

5. Opens every mouth to Praise God

Leadership

Old Covenant	New Covenant
Religion	Relationship
You must.	Will you
Condemns.	Convicts
Duty.	Desire
Protocol.	Pleasure
Requirement	Response
Structure	Synergy
Control	Co-operation
Regulated	Released
Judgement	Joy
Curse.	Covenant

Prayer

Old Covenant	New Covenant
Beg.	Declare
Pray hard.	Pray believing
Many words.	Few words
Reactive.	Proactive
Problem focus	Promise Focus
Mostly asking	Mostly thanking
God reluctant	God is good
Worship prepares prayer	Worship is prayer
Fasting is an event	Fasting lifestyle
Burdened	Joyful
Laugh rarely	Laugh often
Focus on duty.	Focus on intimacy
Expect Spiritual attack's	Expect favour

About the Author

Mark Curtis is the founder and leader of PFJ Ministries, a global network of Churches and Ministries committed to Church Planting, Mission, Training and Church Unity. He is married to Alyson and is a father and grandfather. He loves coffee, Hull City and all things Italian.

About PFJ Ministries

PFJ is a global network that has reached into 80 different nations. PFJ is committed to seeing 100 Churches planted in the UK, 10,000 leaders trained and 1million people saved. What others say about PFJ Ministries

"Mark and PFJ really live up to the name of Passion for Jesus. In a day of focus on flash over substance, PFJ stands out above the crowd as a light shining on a hill. They have a genuine hunger for the 'real' from God and will settle for nothing less. I highly recommend Mark and PFJ to you - you will be blessed."

David Tomberlin, David Tomberlin Ministries

"Passion for Jesus Ministries has at its heart a desire to make Jesus known in the everyday life of people. By touching communities with compassionate acts of kindness and by sharing the passionate stories of God with people, lives are changed and churches planted.

Mark and his team love Jesus, believe in His power to bring hope to the broken and know God still works today."

Rachel Hickson, Heartcry for Change

"It has been said that a name denotes a nature and Passion for Jesus certainly lives up to its name. Not only do they have a strong passion for Jesus but also for the nations. Their commitment to seeing the Kingdom established in the nations is refreshing. I highly recommend them to you."

Duane White, Bridge Church, Denton and O2 Network